ARGUING EUTHANASIA

The Controversy over Mercy Killing, Assisted Suicide, and the "Right to Die"

Edited by
Jonathan D. Moreno, Ph.D.

A Touchstone Book
Published by SIMON & SCHUSTER

New York London Toronto
Sydney Tokyo Singapore

TOUCHSTONE
Rockefeller Center
1230 Avenue of the Americas
New York, NY 10020

Designed by Elina D. Nudelman

Manufactured in the United States of America

10 9 8 7 6 5 4 3 2 1

Library of Congress Cataloging-in-Publication Data

Arguing euthanasia : the controversy over mercy killing, assisted
    suicide, and the "right to die" / edited by Jonathan D. Moreno.
        p.   cm.
    "A Touchstone book."
    1. Euthanasia—Moral and ethical aspects.   2. Right to
die—Moral and ethical aspects.   3. Assisted suicide—Moral
and ethical aspects.   I. Moreno, Jonathan D.
R726.A74   1995
179'.7—dc20
                                                        95-9581
                                                          CIP

ISBN 0-684-80760-2

PERMISSIONS

CONTENTS

8   Contents

Contents 9

INTRODUCTION
Jonathan D. Moreno

In 1974, several months before my twenty-second birthday, my mother and I were forced to make some agonizing decisions. My father, then in his mid-eighties, collapsed following an epidemic of the flu. During the next few weeks he became more and more disoriented, the result of a series of tiny strokes that he had suffered over a period of time but whose cumulative effects were gradually overcoming his recuperative powers. Finally, he stopped eating, and drank only enough to keep his mouth moist.

My father was a physician, and he and my mother had made a pact that, should he become seriously ill, she would not send him to the hospital to die. His wishes stemmed from fifty years of professional experience with large institutions and from his distress at the hospital death of his mother some years before. Fortunately, we were in a position to honor his preference. Early in his illness we installed a hospital bed in his room so that he would not fall while sleeping. Nursing care was available around the clock.

As my father's condition worsened, however, his discomfort grew. Barely coherent, he seemed to reverse his earlier wishes and began asking to be taken to the hospital. At that point his private physician, an old friend and colleague, determined that he was terminally ill and suggested that he be given regular morphine injections. When his doctor asked him if he wanted morphine he shook his head, but he continued to complain of discomfort. The next day, we urged his doctor to give him the injection without asking. Though conscious, this time my father acquiesced to what would be the first of many such injections. Finally he became composed and comfortable, and a few weeks later he passed away quietly.

Our own uncertainty had added to the trauma of the situation. When his pain became intense and he asked to go to the hospital, we had to decide whether this was an authentic request or rather a cry for help. Believing that she knew his true wishes, my mother tried first to relieve his pain. But his initial reluctance to be medicated raised other questions: Did he fear the further clouding of his intellect? Or, in his deluded state, did he think he was being given an overdose? Or did he perhaps simply fail to recognize his old colleague? The decision to proceed with the injection the next day was also fraught with danger: What if he physically resisted? Would we have him restrained and injected against his apparent will, on the grounds that he was confused and deluded? We were trying to help him, but would a second attempt at injection make him less trusting of us in his final days?

Although the story of my father's death seems straightforward in retrospect, at several points it could have gone very differently. If my father had been admitted to the hospital, if his doctor had expressed reluctance about pain medication, or if we had not suggested a more aggressive approach to the injection, his course would have drastically changed. Today it is less likely that a physician would be willing to take care of such a patient outside the hospital— for medical, practical, and legal reasons. But my father knew that his chances of dying peacefully would have been lessened in the hospital. Though technical interventions were limited then, as compared to twenty years later, my father did not want to spend his last days in an impersonal institutional environment. Today, routine end-of-life hospital care tends to be even more aggressive than it was then. In fact, after his suffering was under control, my father gave no indication that he wanted to leave our home or that he wanted the medication to cease. In the time that followed, a legion of old friends and former students were able to visit and say good-bye, unimpeded by hospital technology or visiting hours.

That my father's dying unfolded as it did was due to several factors: his communication of his wishes to my mother, the availability of medical and nursing care at home, the financial wherewithal to afford such services, my mother's exceptional courage and determination, and an era when institutionalized and technologically mediated death could be more easily avoided. Even as recently as the mid-1970s, physicians were less inclined to practice defensive medicine for legal reasons, and end-of-life technology could not so effectively extend the dying process. There was also a measure of luck: We knew him well enough to assess his true wishes accurately when we needed to. I have often wondered how differently things would have gone if any one of these factors had been absent.

I have wondered, too, if we made the right decision in the first place about keeping him at home. Should we have hospitalized him in spite of his previously expressed wish? In doing so we might have had him for a few more months, though in an increasingly debilitated condition. Or, if he was ready to die, would he have preferred to have his trusted medical friend end it quickly with a lethal dose? Or, as a strong-willed man, would he have elected to give himself the injection when still able to do it? As a licensed physician he had access to the medication for an overdose, but considering my father's zest for life, I am sure he never considered death by his own hand. Perhaps he would have preferred his doctor to give him a lethal injection, as in the case of his medical school lecturer Sigmund Freud. Even under the best of circumstances, dying can be a grueling and laborious affair. At one point he said to my mother, after weeks spent lying in bed, "It takes a long time to die."

Mainly I feel that we did well by my father, but doubt is a humane and noble thing when the stakes are so high.

As much as any other personal factor, the experience of my father's dying led me to a career as a teacher and scholar of medical ethics. The subject of euthanasia and assisted suicide is among the most ancient and important in this field. The Hippocratic Oath, which remains the primary touchstone of medical ethics in our culture, appears to rule out physician-assisted death. But it is reasonable to ask how a code that is over two thousand years old can apply to medical techniques that would have been beyond the wildest dreams of its author. In fact, for a few hundred years, and perhaps longer, some patients have called the strict Hippocratic prohibition into question, and it is certain that some doctors have violated it.

Of course, it is one thing to say that a moral code like the Hippocratic Oath is often violated and quite another thing to say that it is wrong. But the fact is that the oath is among the most revered and least read documents of Western civilization, even among physicians. Many medical school commencements include a ritualistic recitation of the oath by the young men and women about to become doctors of medicine, but it is usually a sanitized version that omits references to sensitive subjects like euthanasia and abortion. Ignorance of the Hippocratic Oath's actual content is perhaps best exemplified by the frequent references to the maxim *Primum non nocere*, or "First do no harm." The precept is indeed Hippocratic, but it does not appear in the oath.

One could argue that our modern technology and our complex society have left the oath's ancient wisdom far behind, that what worked twenty-three hundred years ago cannot work now. But even then the Hippocratic circle was but one of many medical cults; and dissatisfaction with its apparent prohibition of physician-assisted suicide, or active euthanasia, is nothing new. In his *Utopia* (1516), Thomas More wrote:

> They console the incurably ill by sitting and talking with them and by alleviating whatever pain they can. Should life become unbearable for these incurables the magistrates and priests do not hesitate to prescribe euthanasia. . . . When the sick have been persuaded of this, they end their lives willingly either by starvation or drugs, that dissolve their lives without any sensation of death. Still, the Utopians do not do away with anyone without his permission, nor lessen any of their duties to him.

Of course, the social conditions under which most people get sick and die are still far short of utopia, which gives rise to legitimate concerns about the implications of such a practice in the real world.

It is interesting that the modern secular state has mainly avoided the issue. Euthanasia and assisted suicide have usually been treated as forms of homicide, at least technically, and only in the Netherlands have the courts officially tolerated the practice. But all that changed dramatically on November 8, 1994, when Oregon voters became the first in the nation to approve a ballot measure that allows doctors to hasten the death of those who are terminally ill. Measure 16 was the successor to two closely defeated initiatives in Washington State in 1991 and in California (for the second time) in 1992. Importantly, those previous efforts permitted a doctor to administer lethal drugs, while the Oregon law only allows a physician to prescribe an overdose of medication. If Measure 16 survives a constitutional challenge in court, it would legalize physician-assisted suicide in Oregon, not active euthanasia, and this is thought to be less liable to abuse. In the Netherlands, allegations that some patients have been put to death without their consent are the basis for powerful criticisms of the Dutch courts' toleration of active euthanasia.

With the approval of the Oregon initiative, an epochal legal, cultural, and psychological barrier has been breached, for better or for worse. Evaluation of the actual results of the law will surely take years, but it may take far less time for other states to approve similar measures, now that the line has been crossed. It is critical to understand how we arrived at this Northwest passage.

The popular movement that led up to the Oregon referendum can be dated from at least 1988, when the *Journal of the American Medical Association* published an anonymous five-hundred-word article called "It's Over, Debbie." The author claimed to be a physician in graduate training who had granted the apparent wish of a seemingly dying young woman to be put out of her misery.

The brief entry unleashed a firestorm of criticism from some of the country's leading medical ethicists, perhaps especially those who were physicians. Their outrage was directed primarily at the reported conduct of the doctor. According to the article, he or she had met this patient only minutes before the event, and in the middle of the night, without even a modicum of standard assessment and consultation. In the critics' judgment, the act described was without the slightest shred of professionalism—a thoughtless murder perpetrated against a vulnerable person in a hospital bed, in wholesale violation of the most elementary standards of medical ethics. The ethicists unleashed a secondary volley at the editor of the prestigious journal for even having published such a document.

A backlash ensued among professionals and members of the general public who were unimpressed by the alleged wisdom of these ethicists; they upbraided the ethics experts for failing to take adequate account of the suffering of the dying. During the 1980s, many people had become sensitized to the contemporary problems of dying. Indeed, stories about dying people had almost become a literary genre. Among them was journalist Betty Rollin's powerful description, in her book *Last Wish*, of her mother's struggle with terminal cancer, and of her decision to assist in her mother's suicide. There were also well-publicized double suicides by aging couples, including that of cultural critic Arthur Koestler, author of *Darkness at Noon,* and his wife.

If the ethicists felt themselves to be taking a principled, even if not wholly popular, stand in the "Debbie" case, there were soon further frontal assaults on the conventional wisdom. Timothy Quill, a respected Rochester, New York, physician, reported in the *New England Journal of Medicine* that he had prescribed barbiturates to a woman suffering from cancer, knowing that she intended to use them to commit suicide. There was nothing anonymous about this report, and unlike the Debbie case, which struck some as a hoax designed to spur discussion, Quill's story about "Diane" had the ring of truth. Most challenging to the prevailing wisdom was the fact that Quill had a long-term professional relationship with Diane and that she had been found free of clinical depression, both thought to be key factors in any justifiable physician-assisted suicide (typically accomplished by the patient's using prescription medication authorized by the cooperating doctor). In contrast, Debbie was the subject of active euthanasia—accomplished in a deliberate and lethal act by the physician. Debbie was not only actively killed but many psychiatrists pointed out that she might have been clinically depressed and therefore unable to rationally assess her situation. On the whole, Quill's approach struck many physicians as the least objectionable form of physician-assisted death; this rendered it a respectable option for some patients.

The growing public debate was further inflamed and complicated by the controversial publication of *Final Exit* by Derek Humphry. Humphry is the founder of the Hemlock Society, an organization that advocates making the option of suicide available to all who suffer and wish to end their lives. A how-to suicide manual, *Final Exit* quickly became a best-seller that put the basics of relatively efficient self-destruction into the hands of nonphysicians.

Then, as if on cue, a retired pathologist named Jack Kevorkian designed a Rube Goldberg–style "suicide machine" that he made available to numbers of persons who were suffering from progressive terminal diseases such as Alzheimer's. The fact that Kevorkian held a medical degree somewhat obscured the fact that his technique was more a matter of engineering than of clinical sophistication. But each of Kevorkian's assisted deaths grabbed headlines. His court battles and jail time transformed him into an odd sort of folk hero who symbolized a populist protest against the medical-legal bureaucracy that seems to stand between the individual and his or her freedom of choice. To many, Kevorkian's was the ultimate act of fighting city hall.

Ironically, the capstone of an evolving moral consensus on end-of-life treatment, the U. S. Supreme Court's decision in the case of Nancy Cruzan, occurred just as this highly publicized and hotly controversial series of incidents was getting under way. Cruzan was a young Missouri woman who had sustained a traumatic head injury in an automobile accident. She survived for years in a "persistent vegetative state" (PVS), the same condition into which Karen Quinlan had lapsed. Patients who are PVS have lost the neurophysiological basis for consciousness. They have sleep-wake cycles and open their eyes, and sometimes they moan, but they have no awareness of their surroundings or of themselves. Their reactions to the world are based entirely on reflex.

Nancy Cruzan's parents wanted to withdraw the feeding tubes that were keeping their daughter alive—unlike the Quinlans, who asked only for the removal of the artificial breathing apparatus. The Cruzans believed that their daughter would not have wanted to be kept alive in this way. They appealed to the Missouri courts to permit them to satisfy what they believed would have been Nancy Cruzan's wish, to be permitted to die, but the state's supreme court ruled that the available evidence was not clear and convincing about Nancy Cruzan's preferences—the standard of evidence required in Missouri in such a case.

The Cruzans decided to appeal the decision to the U.S. Supreme Court, which delivered its ruling in 1990.

In *Cruzan* the Supreme Court upheld a state's right to require a high standard of evidence about an incompetent patient's previous wishes concerning life-sustaining treatment. Though that decision was regarded as a setback by some patients' rights advocates, the justices also articulated the well-recognized right of a competent patient to decline any and all treatment, including life-sustaining treatment. This was a first for the high court. Further, from a legal point of view, the justices settled a question that had been a hot spot of medical ethics debate in the 1980s—whether artificial feeding counted as a form of medical therapy that (like a ventilator) could be declined in advance. The court concluded that feeding tubes are a high-tech treatment that may not be forced on a patient, even though the obvious outcome will be starvation.

The Cruzans lost the battle but won the war. Back home, a court-appointed guardian for Nancy determined that new information about her wishes was indeed clear and convincing. The feeding tubes were removed and Nancy Cruzan died. The critical point in the aftermath of *Cruzan* is this: the legal right to decline life-sustaining treatment after one is no longer conscious clearly applies to artificial feeding. This landmark decision appears to certify that, in the United States, patients may decline any and all life-sustaining treatment, even if they become unconscious—a legal right that can be accepted even by those who reject active euthanasia or physician-assisted suicide.

To many in the medical ethics community, the undisciplined public debate about euthanasia that arose around the time of the court's decision threatened to disrupt the carefully wrought consensus, culminating in *Cruzan*, about patients' rights to forgo life-sustaining treatment. Though these rights had long been recognized in the common law for competent patients, clinical realities often involve patients like Nancy Cruzan who have lost the capacity to decide. Progress toward the emerging doctrine that *formerly competent* patients did not lose this right had effectively begun with the *Quinlan* decision in 1976, which assured the right of a permanently unconscious patient to forgo artificial breathing. A presidential commission on ethical problems in medicine strongly concurred in 1982, and this is the view that crystallized decisively in *Cruzan*.

But now, after all this work to assure the rights of patients who are no longer competent to forgo end-of-life treatment, some worried that the clamor for more active control over dying would both obscure and jeopardize the real progress that had been made. In fact, the state of Michigan enacted a statute, aimed at Kevorkian, that many thought went too far by inhibiting appropriate patient decisions to forgo treatment.

Strictly speaking, the term "euthanasia" refers to actions or omissions that result in the death of a person who is already gravely ill. Techniques of active euthanasia range from gunfire to lethal injection, while passive euthanasia can be achieved by failing to treat a pneumonia or by withholding or withdrawing ventilatory support. The current medical ethics consensus has thus implicitly legitimized *voluntary* passive euthanasia. This consensus relies on the moral legitimacy of letting the underlying disease process take its natural course, if that is what the patient would have wanted. Although many do not find passive euthanasia to satisfy the idea of a "good death" (eu-thanasia), most prefer it to lengthening the dying process due to human intervention.

Yet this consensus is fairly narrow, and at its margins there are problems. Although passive euthanasia against the patient's wishes *(involuntary)* is clearly prohibited by the current consensus, passive euthanasia in the absence of knowledge of the patient's wishes *(nonvoluntary)* remains controversial. Also, some acts of euthanasia are hard to classify. Some of those who can accept withdrawal of ventilatory support if wanted by the patient (a clear case of passive voluntary euthanasia) nevertheless reject the withdrawal of feeding tubes, even at the patient's request. In spite of the Supreme Court's decision in *Cruzan*, this difference of opinion is not likely to disappear.

Within the meaning of *active* euthanasia, the difference between *voluntary* euthanasia and *nonvoluntary* euthanasia is also important. Active voluntary euthanasia is performed at the patient's request, while active nonvoluntary euthanasia may be performed on a patient who is not competent and who has not requested it. There is also active *involuntary* euthanasia, which refers to "mercy killing" done against the patient's wishes. Although hardly anyone advocates active involuntary euthanasia, some worry that we are on the "slippery slope" to such exterminations, perhaps on a Nazilike, eugenic basis. In any case, when advocates talk about euthanasia, they can generally be assumed to mean the kind that is voluntary, with the passive variety far less controversial than the active. And all those who advocate that dying patients should be permitted to die when they wish endorse assisted suicide.

In spite of the ethicists' conviction that the humane abatement of life-sustaining treatment can and should be kept distinct from the active-euthanasia and assisted-suicide debate, their critics assert that the drift toward more deliberate means of ending life is a natural consequence of the slippery slope represented in the triumph of autonomy. In reply, it should be pointed out that our society has in fact clambered *up* the slope, toward greater scrutiny of end-of-life treatment than was true a generation ago, when most Americans died under the supervision of doctors who were left largely to their own devices. In those days, passive euthanasia, with or without knowledge of the patient's wishes, was probably far more common than it is today. Many senior physicians recall cases of dying elderly patients who could not feed themselves but were comfortable. It was regarded as inhumane to force-feed them and extend their dying process. Instead, a glass of water was placed next to their night table with the rationale, "If she wants to take a drink, she will."

Yet slippery slopes cannot easily be dismissed in an era when the boundaries of life are being technologically challenged at both ends. Human life with test tube origins is now a commonplace. We will shortly be in a position not only to avoid giving birth to children with certain terrible afflictions but also to design individuals with genetically engineered desirable characteristics. Try as we might to set limits on future manipulations of chromosomes, the genies of applied science are notoriously difficult to put back into their lamps, as the atomic age attests. One simply cannot predict whether, or how, a society with so much control over the beginning of life will seek to control its end.

Clearly, the recent euthanasia debate has incorporated a wider subject area than euthanasia *per se*. Assisted suicide, and especially physician-assisted suicide, has come within the ambit of the controversy, even though it does not fall within the strict meaning of "euthanasia," and even though the term "suicide" has pejorative implications that "euthanasia" does not have. Although one might object to this development on semantic grounds, it does reflect the fact that modern medical interventions have themselves obscured the difference between euthanasia and suicide. Take the example of a competent patient with end-stage emphysema. If she insists on the cessation of ventilatory support, is that euthanasia or suicide? Moreover, if a decision is made to medicate the patient so that she does not experience suffocation, is that appropriate therapy or physician-assisted suicide?

Advances in life-sustaining technology include ventilators, artificial feeding, and advanced cardiac life support. There have also been vast improvements in life-*extending* technologies, such as cancer chemotherapy and, allegedly, the drug AZT for AIDS. Although the life-extending therapies are not usually directly implicated in euthanasia debates, they have created a novel sort of dependence on the medical system previously unknown to patients who were, in some sense, dying. Thus, some have asserted that a physician has an obligation to do more than cease providing such treatment when the patient wishes it to stop; after all, the patient's life has been extended by this intervention, and so has his suffering. Shouldn't the physician then advance the moment of death at the patient's request, and if she refuses, isn't this a form of abandonment?

In part, this aspect of the debate has turned on a disagreement about the ways in which dying patients actually suffer and the extent to which that suffering can be alleviated. Those who object to the termination of food and fluids argue that no one should undergo starvation, while experts in hospice care contend that, properly managed, this is among the least uncomfortable ways to die. Those who object to abandoning a terminal cancer patient to the disease's natural end stage note the pain she will endure, while experts in palliative care claim that proper pain management can be applied to all but the most intractable cases, without resort to active euthanasia.

The moral significance of a dying person's pain has also been subject to philosophical disagreement. The philosopher James Rachels famously argued that active euthanasia may actually be morally preferable to passive euthanasia if the patient will suffer during a drawn-out process of natural death. Others have wondered how broadly the idea of pain should be construed: Does the knowledge that one is facing a gradually degenerative course, as in the case of amyotrophic lateral sclerosis (Lou Gehrig's disease), create so much mental suffering that this is a rational reason to consider suicide? What about the person suffering from years of chronic depression that has proven refractory to treatment?

The question of whether a suicide can ever be rational falls into the boundary of psychiatry and philosophy. In general, the two literatures agree that, while suicide hardly ever meets the criteria of rationality, it cannot be ruled out in all cases. Philosophically, a rational assessment of one's prospects might, in theory, yield the calculation that an end to one's life is more valuable (for oneself and for those one loves) than continuing life with burdens that cannot be compensated by other experiences. Psychiatrically, although depression typically accompanies suicidal ideation, it cannot be said always to accompany such thoughts. In any case, even if the suicidal act does not meet the highest standards of rationality, the contention that one has a moral *right* to suicide is different: Whose life is it anyway?

In the largest sense, the euthanasia debate has been energized in the modern world by the insistence in recent medical ethics on patient self-determination. The abortion debate, too, reflects the influence of the self-determination principle. Abortion may also share with euthanasia the distinction of being one of the most ancient medical ethics issues, given the explicit mention of both in most versions of the Hippocratic Oath. The euthanasia debate differs from the conflict over abortion in crucial ways, however: It has not been so extremely and, perhaps, hopelessly politicized as abortion, and it does not involve allegations of a second, innocent life. Rather, euthanasia, and especially physician-assisted suicide, appears as the ultimate postmodern demand for personal dignity in an era of technologically mediated death.

If this book succeeds, it will be as a tool for assessing the validity of that demand. The first part, "It's Not Over Yet, Debbie," can be read as the practical beginning of the contemporary debate. "Through Doctors' Eyes" presents the human picture through the eyes of two humane but differing physicians. Part Three, "The Dutch Model," not only provides our only model for legally tolerated euthanasia but takes on deeper significance in light of the successful Oregon referendum. "Northwest Passage" highlights the current political atmosphere in which the debate has taken place. And the final section raises questions for the future, questions that may perhaps be answered only through precedent and experience.

If I could commend one critical question to the reader, it would be this: Given both the inevitability of death and the fact that human arrangements rarely satisfy human aspirations, can a system of physician-assisted dying satisfy individual preferences without degrading values that are abstract but of continuing importance? Put differently: Are there circumstances under which assisted suicide or euthanasia would leave unharmed, if not promote, life-oriented values?

Nietzsche thought so. In *Zarathustra*, the grandfather of postmodernism had his prophet declare his determination not to be like the "rope makers," who "drag out their threads behind them." Zarathustra called for a "free death," the only one that can "hallow the oaths of the living."

But there is another side of the Nietzschean tradition besides that of personal transcendence. Whether justly or not, for modern readers references to Nietzsche are often reminders of holocausts against defenseless innocents, and none is more vulnerable than the dying person. That vulnerability works both ways, of course: vulnerable to suffering as well as to harm. Some acts intended to prevent suffering may inadvertently cause still greater harm. Does euthanasia fall into that category? Or assisted suicide? I cannot think of a greater challenge to our wisdom or our humanity.

Part I

IT'S NOT OVER YET, DEBBIE

When the highly respected *Journal of the American Medical Association (JAMA)* published the brief item "It's Over, Debbie" in 1988, it sparked a firestorm of criticism. The euthanasia debate had been heating up for some time, but "Debbie" placed it squarely in the hospital context and on the doctors' shoulders. It should be emphasized that the "Debbie" scenario is one of active euthanasia, not physician-assisted suicide, because the young doctor in the piece actually administered the lethal dose, not the patient. To many people this makes a very big difference.

In "Doctors Must Not Kill," four influential physician-ethicists attack not only the sentiment expressed in "It's Over, Debbie" but even the decision to publish the piece in the first place. To them, *JAMA* was in effect legitimizing the irresponsible outer reaches of the assisted-suicide position. Elements of "Debbie" suggested to some that it was really a hoax—for instance, the reference to the archaic and useless alcohol drip. But these authors argue that, on its face, the piece constitutes evidence that a homicide had been committed and should be investigated by the authorities. In any case, they conclude, it is always wrong for a doctor to kill a patient under any circumstances.

The theologian and medical ethicist Kenneth Vaux also condemns the "Debbie" scenario but urges that it not be used as an excuse for doctors to prolong the dying process and the suffering that may accompany it. Vaux is willing to allow physician-assisted suicide under certain "exceptional" cases that are expressions of compassion for the patient.

The last item in this part, by philosopher-physician H. Tristram Engelhardt Jr., places the debate about "Debbie" in its broader social and political context. Consider these two questions: In a society in which free men and women are supposed to be reluctant to impose their values on one another, who can say what is wrong? May the state impose a particular vision of the good life, and of the good death?

Perhaps, though, these two questions are more different than they at first appear. If so, then the euthanasia debate is ultimately about ethics, not about law.

It's Over, Debbie

Anonymous

This unsigned piece appeared in *JAMA* in 1988. The author, who represents herself or himself as a resident on call, tells a disturbing story. Whether a report of an authentic situation or not, this short item focused the attention of the medical profession as few other recent publications have.

The call came in the middle of the night. As a gynecology resident rotating through a large, private hospital, I had come to detest telephone calls, because invariably I would be up for several hours and would not feel good the next day. However, duty called, so I answered the phone. A nurse informed me that a patient was having difficulty getting rest, could I please see her. She was on 3 North. That was the gynecologic-oncology unit, not my usual duty station. As I trudged along, bumping sleepily against walls and corners and not believing I was up again, I tried to imagine what I might find at the end of my walk. Maybe an elderly woman with an anxiety reaction, or perhaps something particularly horrible.

I grabbed the chart from the nurses station on my way to the patient's room, and the nurse gave me some hurried details: a 20-year-old girl named Debbie was dying of ovarian cancer. She was having unrelenting vomiting apparently as the result of an alcohol drip administered for sedation. Hmmm, I thought. Very sad. As I approached the room I could hear loud, labored breathing. I entered and saw an emaciated, dark-haired woman who appeared much older than 20. She was receiving nasal oxygen, had an IV, and was sitting in bed suffering from what was obviously severe air hunger. The chart noted her weight at 80 pounds. A second woman, also dark-haired but of middle age, stood at her right, holding her hand. Both looked up as I entered.

The room seemed filled with the patient's desperate effort to survive. Her eyes were hollow, and she had suprasternal and intercostal retractions with her rapid inspirations. She had not eaten or slept in two days. She had not responded to chemotherapy and was being given supportive care only. It was a gallows scene, a cruel mockery of her youth and unfulfilled potential. Her only words to me were, "Let's get this over with."

I retreated with my thoughts to the nurses station. The patient was tired and needed rest. I could not give her health, but I could give her rest. I asked the nurse to draw 20 mg of morphine sulfate into a syringe. Enough, I thought, to do the job. I took the syringe into the room and told the two women I was going to give Debbie something that would let her rest and to say good-bye. Debbie looked at the syringe, then laid her head on the pillow with her eyes open, watching what was left of the world. I injected the morphine intravenously and watched to see if my calculations on its effects would be correct. Within seconds her breathing slowed to a normal rate, her eyes closed, and her features softened as she seemed restful at last. The older woman stroked the hair of the now-sleeping patient. I waited for the inevitable next effect of depressing the respiratory drive. With clocklike certainty, within four minutes the breathing rate slowed even more, then became irregular, then ceased. The dark-haired woman stood erect and seemed relieved.

It's over, Debbie.

Doctors Must Not Kill

Willard Gaylin, Leon R. Kass, Edmund R. Pellegrino, and Mark Siegler

These four distinguished physician-ethicists joined to
write this response to "It's Over, Debbie." Willard Gaylin recently retired as board chairman of the Hastings
Center, of which he was the cofounder. Leon R. Kass is
a professor in the Committee on Social Thought and in
the College of the University of Chicago. Edmund R.
Pellegrino is a professor at the Georgetown University
School of Medicine and directs its clinical ethics program. Mark Siegler is a professor at the University of
Chicago medical school and is the director of the bioethics center there.

In the middle of the night, a sleepy gynecology resident is
called to attend a young woman, dying of cancer, whom
he has never seen before. Horrified by her severe distress,
and proceeding alone without consultation with anyone, he
gives her a lethal injection of morphine, clearly intending
the death that promptly ensues. The resident submits a
first-person account of his killing to the *Journal of the
American Medical Association*. Without any editorial comment, *JAMA* publishes the account, withholding the author's name at his request. What in the world is going on?

Before the sophisticated obscure our vision with clouds of
arguments and subtle qualifications, we must fix our gaze
on the brute facts.

First, on his own admission, the resident appears to have
committed a felony: premeditated murder. Direct intentional homicide is a felony in all American jurisdictions, for
which the plea of merciful motive is no excuse. That the
homicide was clearly intentional is confirmed by the resident's act of unrepentant publication.

Second, law aside, the physician behaved altogether in a scandalously unprofessional and unethical manner. He did not know the patient: he had never seen her before, he did not study her chart, he did not converse with her or her family. He never spoke to *her* physician. He took as an unambiguous command her only words to him, "Let's get this over with": he did not bother finding out what precisely she meant or whether she meant it wholeheartedly. He did not consider alternative ways of bringing her relief or comfort; instead of comfort, he gave her death. This is no humane and thoughtful physician succumbing with fear and trembling to the pressures and well-considered wishes of a patient well known to him, for whom there was truly no other recourse. This is, by his own account, an impulsive yet cold technician, arrogantly masquerading as a knight of compassion and humanity. (Indeed, so cavalier is the report and so cold-blooded the behavior, it strains our credulity to think that the story is true.)

Third, law and professional manner both aside, the resident violated one of the first and most hallowed canons of the medical ethic: doctors must not kill. Generations of physicians and commentators on medical ethics have underscored and held fast to the distinction between ceasing useless treatments (or allowing to die) and active, willful taking of life; at least since the Oath of Hippocrates, Western medicine has regarded the killing of patients, even on request, as a profound violation of the deepest meaning of the medical vocation. As recently as 1986, the Judicial Council of the American Medical Association, in an opinion regarding treatment of dying patients, affirmed the principle that a physician "should not intentionally cause death." Neither legal tolerance nor the best bedside manner can ever make medical killing medically ethical.

The conduct of the physician is inexcusable. But the conduct of the editor of *JAMA* is incomprehensible. By publishing this report, he knowingly publicizes a felony and shields the felon. He deliberately publicizes the grossest medical malfeasance and shields the malefactor from professional scrutiny and judgment, presumably allowing him to continue his practices without possibility of rebuke and remonstrance, not even from the physician whose private patient he privately dispatched. Why? For what possible purpose central to *JAMA*'s professional mission?

According to newspaper reports, the editor of *JAMA* published the article "to promote discussion" of a timely and controversial topic. But is this a responsible way for the prestigious voice of our venerable profession to address the subject of medical killing? Is it morally responsible to promulgate challenges to our most fundamental moral principles without editorial rebuke or comment, "for the sake of discussion"? Decent folk do not deliberately stir discussion of outrageous practices, like slavery, incest, or killing those in our care.

What is to be done? Regarding the case at hand, the proper course is clear. *JAMA* should voluntarily turn all the information it has regarding the case over to the legal authorities in the pertinent jurisdictions. The physician's name should also be reported to his hospital directors and to his state and county medical societies for their scrutiny and action. The Council on Ethical and Judicial Affairs of the American Medical Association should examine the case, as well as the decision to publish it. Justice requires nothing less.

But much more is at stake than punishing an offender. The very soul of medicine is on trial. For this is not one of those peripheral issues about which pluralism and relativism can be tolerated, about which a value-free stand on the substance can be hedged around with procedural safeguards to ensure informed consent or "sound decision-making." Nor is this an issue, like advertising, fee-splitting, or cooperation with chiropractors, that touches medicine only as a trade. This issue touches medicine at its very moral center; if this moral center collapses, if physicians become killers or are even merely licensed to kill, the profession—and, therewith, each physician—will never again be worthy of trust and respect as healer and comforter and protector of life in all its frailty. For if medicine's power over life may be used equally to heal or to kill, the doctor is no more a moral professional but rather a morally neutered technician.

These are perilous times for our profession. The Hemlock Society and others are in the courts and legislatures trying to legalize killing by physicians at patient request. Such a proposal is almost certainly going to be on the ballot in California next November. High costs of care for the old and incurable already tempt some physicians to regard as "dispensable" some patients who never express the wish to die. In the Netherlands, where barriers to physician killing are gone, there are now many well-documented cases of such cryptic and "uninvited" killing by doctors.

Now is not the time for promoting neutral discussion. Rather, now is the time for the medical profession to rally in defense of its fundamental moral principles, to repudiate any and all acts of direct and intentional killing by physicians and their agents. We call on the profession and its leadership to obtain the best advice, regarding both theory and practice, about how to defend the profession's moral center and to resist growing pressures both from without and from within. We call on fellow physicians to say that we will not deliberately kill. We must say also to each of our fellow physicians that we will not tolerate killing of patients and that we will take disciplinary action against doctors who kill. And we must say to the broader community that if it insists on tolerating or legalizing active euthanasia, it will have to find nonphysicians to do its killing.

Debbie's Dying:
Mercy Killing and the Good Death

Kenneth L. Vaux

Kenneth L. Vaux is a well-known theologian and bio-ethicist. He is professor of ethics in medicine at the University of Illinois, Champagne-Urbana. This piece in response to "It's Over, Debbie" also appeared first in *JAMA* in 1988.

Most of the condemnatory response to "It's Over, Debbie" has rightly claimed that what (apparently) transpired that night was unconscionable. One does not stumble angrily into the night and decide profound matters of life and death for another human being. This strange narrative does not tell us whether Debbie wanted simply to be relieved of pain or released from intolerable suffering; whether the family consented or what the nurses or chaplains on call advised; or whether the attending or primary physician, if one existed, authorized the action. The whole process, from beginning to end, was morally unacceptable.

A deeper question, however, lies behind the widespread interest in this one reprehensible action—the question that troubles us all. As I lie dying, will I be offered humane care, will I be done in too soon by some expediency, or will I be subjected to terminal torture?

Euthanasia does not refer to Nazi-like elimination of the sick, old, or unproductive, and, because it lacks any account of patient consent, "It's Over, Debbie" is in no way an accurate representation of any form of euthanasia. Traditionally, euthanasia means the search for a good death, an easier death for one who is dying, a death released in some measure from intractable suffering. It assumes and requires the patient's unequivocal request and the consent of the family. Our best medical and religious traditions

37

accept euthanasia when it assists the person who is imminently dying toward a less devastating and more peaceful demise. Passive euthanasia *often,* double-effect euthanasia *sometimes,* and active euthanasia *rarely* have become established as a morally acceptable continuum of action in our ethical tradition.

One reading of this ambiguous and melodramatic diary suggests that Debbie's case may be one of *double-effect* euthanasia: the patient died as a result of medication given in an attempt to relieve pain and with the knowledge that it would hasten death. Morphine is not normally a poison but an analgesic drug, and 20 mg is scarcely a murderous dose. The physician could not possibly have known with the brash confidence that his narrative displays that his injection would kill. More likely, he sought to provide relief and rest to this dying young woman, knowing that it would speed her death. In the pursuit of a legitimate, indeed obligatory, purpose of relieving suffering, he shortened the remaining hours of her life. If this is a true rendition of Debbie's case, it represents an instance of morally acceptable double-effect euthanasia (or what is technically called *agathanasia,* a better death). The side effect is unfortunate, indeed grievous, but it is not unethical.

The President's Commission report on *Decisions to Forego Life-Sustaining Treatment* and many cancer care texts hold that it is permissible to use analgesic treatment for end-stage cancer pain and respiratory distress even if it hastens death. As the President's Commission [on Ethical Problems in Medicine] report states,

> No death is more agonizing for the aware patient . . . than one from respiration insufficiency. Untreated, the patient will struggle for air until exhausted, when carbon dioxide narcosis and progressive hypoxia finally bring death fairly quickly. With the consent of the family morphine may be given. . . . If the patient is already quite exhausted, the slowed respirations will induce hypercapnia, which will

perpetuate the sedation, and the patient will die in the ensuing sleep.

What about intentional mercy killing—active and direct euthanasia? Is such action ever medically or ethically acceptable? Even if it is proscribed, can it be excused from legal prosecution or professional censure? Down through the ages, when the patient and physician have established a clear understanding and the physician's desire has been to relieve the patient's incurable pain, most cases of mercy killing have been excused by virtue of the spirit rather than the letter of the law. In all noble jurisprudence and even more in the ethics of caring for the dying, absolutist principles must always be chastened by mercy.

I argue that while positive euthanasia must be proscribed in principle, in exceptional cases it may be abided in deed. There has always been a place, albeit carefully restricted to a limited range of cases, for voluntary euthanasia. From classical times throughout the Christian centuries and into modern secular society, this allowance has always existed alongside the dominant ethic of prolonging and sustaining life. There are numerous cases today in the medical and legal case files in which active euthanasia has been reluctantly allowed and the physicians involved have not been prosecuted. In his classic of medical ethics, *The Patient as Person*, Paul Ramsey, PhD, a spokesman for traditional ethics, makes unrelenting cancer pain an exception to the dominant ethic of "doing nothing to place the dying more quickly beyond our love and care." Here, "one can hardly be held morally blameworthy if in these instances dying is directly accomplished or hastened."

Philosophical ethics aside, the most moving evidence I have witnessed for this viewpoint in my 25 years as a consultant in medical ethics is the testimony of highly ethical and humane physicians. Although impeded by law and custom from giving a lethal dose to their patient, these physicians would, in fact, do so even at risk of prosecution for their wife or father or child if the patient was suffering in such end-of-life agony as Debbie.

That physicians and nurses would request euthanasia of their colleagues or would assist their own loved ones to have a more merciful death but would deny it to their patients says something about the moral nature of the act. Such loving acts illustrate a kind of "exception" ethic that has a place in the tradition of alleviating suffering.

The position of "exceptional-case" active euthanasia is grounded in classical clinical wisdom. In the Hippocratic tradition, the physician was discouraged from therapeutically or technologically invading the atrium of death. Attempts to cure had to yield to attempts to comfort. An ethical principle that later transformed Western medicine held that the living ought never to be treated as if they were dying, nor the dying as if they were living. To know the difference entailed discerning the *signum Hippocraticum* (the signs of mortality).

In recent years the qualities that morally distinguished the living from the dying have been blurred. With our life-prolonging techniques and medications, we have transformed death; we have taken it out of the acute, natural, and noninterventional mode and made it more into a chronic, contrived, and manipulated phenomenon. Deaths as inevitable as Debbie's have been protracted by a range of interventions, including chemotherapy (disrupting the cellular-pathogenic process), analgesia (altering the release of natural body endorphins and narcotics), the administration of intravenous fluids and nutrients, and hospitalization itself. Logically and emotionally, we cannot intervene at one phase and then be inactive at another, more painful phase. We cannot modify nature and then plead that nature must be allowed to run its unhindered course.

Medicine is a pastoral art, especially when a good physician, like a good shepherd, accompanies a patient "into the valley of the shadow." Here the dying one must indeed "fear no evil," either the evil of weary dispatch or of principled withdrawal.

Where does this leave us? The outrage of Debbie's case reminds us that we must never abandon the cardinal purpose of medical care—to save and sustain life and never intentionally to harm or kill. The other lesson of this case is that we must not destroy the virtue of that commitment by using medical art to prolong dying and puritanically refuse to relieve suffering. This distortion is very possible today, when technological process is joined to low rates of bed occupancy and economic distress in hospitals and when our society tends to deny the inevitability of death. If biomedical acts of life extension become acts of death prolongation, we may force some patients to outlive their deaths, and we may ultimately repudiate the primary life-saving and merciful ethic itself.

Fashioning an Ethic for Life and Death in a Post-Modern Society

H. Tristram Engelhardt Jr.

Trained as a physician and as a philosopher, H. Tristram Engelhardt Jr. is an influential writer in bioethics with a unique philosphical perspective. His response to "It's Over, Debbie" opens up the wider social and political implications of the episode. Some small changes have been made to the original version, which was pub-lished in the *Hastings Center Report* for January-February 1989.

"It's Over, Debbie" has provoked a cluster of overlapping debates. Some commentators have focused on the general issue of consent and authority to act. The vignette does not indicate whether Debbie asked for, agreed to, or wanted to have her death expedited. Others have been concerned that the role and significance of medicine would be invidiously changed if physicians not only sustained life, but ushered in death. At stake here has been the self-image and the perception by others of what it means to be a physician. There have also been arguments about slippery slopes and the undermining of respect for life. Many if not most of these debates turn on particular concrete understandings of the good life and the good death. But for public policy in a secular pluralist society such as ours, the question is not so much whether voluntary euthanasia is right or wrong, but whether the state may use force to stop competent individuals from being voluntarily euthanatized when they do not have special preempting duties to third parties. This is the question, and only with respect to voluntary euthanasia, I will address.

Much of applied ethics proceeds as if Renaissance and Enlightenment assumptions regarding the nature of ethics and the authority of the state were still firmly established. They are, however, if not irrevocably undermined, at least in substantial jeopardy. This is not to claim that the majority of individuals in fact recognize how weak the moral and conceptual foundations are for much of bioethics and public policy. But what Nietzsche said with regard to the death of God in the nineteenth century is true of much of ethics and political theory in the twentieth. The assumptions on which they are based have long since expired, at least as supports for generally justifiable public policy. There is far from any agreement, or near-agreement, about how one can establish or identify as canonical a particular normative view of the moral life. It is also unclear how one can justify the traditional sweep of authority claimed by the state. Prior to the Enlightenment, the state had been justified in terms of Divine right. But if one is not to appeal to God (and such an appeal would appear out of place for a secular society), then it might appear that one can determine who is a moral authority and who is in moral authority by determining what it is reasonable to do. If one enforces what is reasonable, what reasonable person could find fault?

But the problem is to determine that moral and political agenda which reason would endorse. It will not help to appeal to ideal or disinterested observers. On the one hand, if one chooses a truly disinterested observer, that observer will not be a partisan of any particular concrete moral viewpoint. It will not possess a particular moral sense, which means it will not be useful for definitively identifying any one moral viewpoint. On the other hand, if the ideal observer to whom one appeals can resolve a controversy, this will be because one incorporates a particular content-full moral sense or a commitment to a particular canonical concrete view of proper deportment. This problem of gaining moral content without begging the question plagues all hypothetical choice theories, including those that appeal to hypothetical contractors. Either they are parochial and beg the question, or if they are not parochial, they are morally useless. Intuitionism will not be of any help either, for any given intuition can be met by a contrary one. Nor will an appeal to consequences help; unless one knows how to weigh different consequences, one does not know which outcomes are morally preferable. Neither is there any non-controversial way of reading off from nature canons for human conduct, because all conclusions in such endeavors presuppose a particular sense of nature's significance. Considerations such as these (for example, that choices of thin theories of the good are always arbitrary) have led John Rawls to acknowledge that his view of justice does not have a universal claim on persons, but only on those who have a commitment to a particular view of society.

What does all this have to do with euthanasia? Unless one can establish a canonical concrete view of the good life (and thus of the good death), it may not in principle be possible to decide in general secular terms when and under what circumstances euthanasia is morally opprobrious or praiseworthy, to be forbidden or tolerated. For instance, all may agree (though this assumption itself is controversial) that humans are interested in achieving liberty, equality, prosperity, and security through social cooperation. However, one will not know what society to endorse unless one knows how one should rank these individual and social desiderata. Any serious exploration of the moral probity of euthanasia must first show how one can in principle answer two cardinal questions: When is it good or bad to ask others for assistance in euthanasia?; to provide others with assistance in euthanasia? When may one use state force to prevent individuals from seeking assistance in euthanasia?; to prevent others from providing assistance in euthanasia? If one cannot see how to answer these questions, in general secular terms they cease to be serious philosophical questions and must be regarded as issues of mere political expediency or *Realpolitik*. The philosophical question is: who *may* effectively constrain others so as to impose a particular view of the good life and the good death? And why?

This foundational approach to the problem is unavoidable for more than intellectual reasons: we are a society that is secular and increasingly diverse. In the future it will no longer be plausible to speak of the Judeo-Christian heritage providing a taken-for-granted basis for American life, for we will have an increasingly important representation of Islamic, Hindu, and Buddhist believers. Moreover, as medical technology allows individuals to have their lives prolonged, but often under circumstances that they would find unacceptable, many will find it rational to accept treatment only if they can leave instructions about when they would wish to be euthanatized, should the treatment fail. Moreover, increasing life expectancy will mean that more individuals will close their lives severely senile and requiring expensive custodial care, and many will find it unreasonable to set aside resources for care under such circumstances. Instead, many would rather enjoy the resources now or invest them to help others who can enjoy them, and give instructions to be euthanatized should they become profoundly senile. Decriminalized euthanasia would allow many to choose treatment rationally and to avoid useless costs. For them it will appear senseless that lives that do no good for those who live them may not be terminated on request.

The foregoing are practical issues. They indicate why the problem of euthanasia will not go away, and why from a sociopolitical point of view old solutions will not be plausible. However, the central challenge is intellectual: grounding or establishing a particular ethic regarding euthanasia. With different rankings of values the morality of euthanasia will be understood quite differently. Even if one remains a believing Orthodox Catholic, Jew, or Protestant, eschewing euthanasia on religious grounds (as do I), there will be the challenge of establishing in general terms why a secular society compassing a plurality of moral viewpoints may forbid euthanasia. This latter is not merely a political issue. It is an issue where political philosophy is equivalent to natural law as the attempt to establish at least some generally justifiable moral grounds for coercive state force.

It is, after all, an issue of secular morality as to what the state may forbid through its extensive coercive means.

One might in the end rail against the above, asking why one should be so bent on foundationalism anyway. But, if one cannot establish a generally justifiable warrant for coercive state force, one has abandoned ethics as a general secular endeavor and given up on providing a general moral justification for the coercive endeavors of the state. The difficulty is that, to justify state force, one would hope to show that the behavior the state is enforcing is morally justifiable; that the state has the authority to impose such behavior on the unconsenting; and that the imposition will produce more benefits than harms.

Given the foregoing skepticism regarding the possibility of grounding a secular ethics on the authority of the state, it might appear in principle impossible ever to meet these three conditions. As already noted, appeals to hypothetical choice theories, consequentialism, natural law, intuitions, or any concrete view of proper action seem doomed to failure.

However, there is a quasi-Kantian escape from skepticism and nihilism. Insofar as individuals are interested in resolving issues without recourse to force, they will be able peaceably to create together a moral fabric for their common life. All that needs to be presumed is mutual respect, a commitment not to use others without their consent. On the other hand, should one reject this endeavor, one renounces the possibility of a general morality and therefore cannot protest with a general moral justification when one is used coercively by others. The argument, in short, has a self-referential character. If you want to play the game of ethics, you can create a moral world with others. If you do not want to play the game of ethics, you cannot complain—at least with a general rational warrant. One is not committed to any particular thin theory of the good, to any particular ranking of values in order to play ethics. All one is committed to is not using others without their consent. One is not valuing autonomy but gaining authority and sustaining a secular moral world by seeking the consent of others and by otherwise forbearing from using them. This allows one still to condemn and coerce murderers, rapists, thieves, and those who violate recorded contracts. It allows one to distribute as welfare entitlements the proceeds from commonly owned goods. And it explains why limited democracies and free and informed consent are so important for post-modern man: They are ways of resolving controversies and creating joint societal undertakings even when no common concrete, content-full oral understandings can be discovered, but individuals together wish to fashion a common policy. Limited democracies and free and informed consent are not so much to be justified on the basis of liberal sentiments about the value of freedom, as they are on the basis of the one remaining, generally justifiable strategy for resolving moral disputes with moral authority. They are expressions of the one source of moral authority when it cannot be derived from reason or from God: the consent or agreement of those involved. Where reason fails, the will to peaceable resolution can succeed, but without content.

This is not the place to develop the foundations for a general secular pluralist ethic. All I wish to indicate is that while it is very likely that something can be saved of the Enlightenment endeavor, it is unlikely to be enough to give moral authority to state attempts to forbid euthanasia. Whatever will be saved is unlikely to include a canonical moral ranking of human values. One is likely to get much less from general secular ethics than one had originally hoped. For example, a blanket state-enforced prohibition of euthanasia is unlikely to be justifiable in general secular terms. One may be able to develop traditional arguments for limitations on the right to refuse treatment so as to limit the right to seek assistance in one's death. Duties to dependent minors or undischarged debts as antecedent contracts may provide a basis for morally forbidding euthanasia until one has provided for the minors or discharged the debts. Those obligations are likely to be defeated, leaving one free to act if one is terminal and so ill that such provisions cannot be made. Similarly, moral limits may be placed on the right of the non–terminally ill to seek assistance or to be aided in ending their lives by special obligations such as those of a spouse or a member of the military.

But beyond such special obligations, it is unlikely that one will be able to establish that citizens have relinquished control over their own lives by being members of a large-scale state so as not to be morally free to seek euthanasia. The notion of society as a vehicle for the peaceable resolution of controversies, the protection of contracts, and the distribution of proceeds from common resources does not commit one to the state having the moral authority to stop competent individuals from contracting for euthanasia, unless there are special duties to third persons. The point is that one cannot meet the three conditions for justified state authority sketched above. First, one will not be able to show in general secular terms that it is wrong for competent individuals to end their lives with or without the assistance of others, if those individuals do not have special duties to third parties. To establish that it would be wrong would require establishing a hierarchy of values that subordinates the value of individual liberty to other special social values. However, if one cannot discover a canonical ranking of values, then one cannot establish in general secular terms whether it would be right or wrong to end one's life in the absence of special countervening duties. As a result, one could not establish that the state, in acting to forbid euthanasia, would be acting rightly. Moreover, if the very notion of the social contract or of the state does not include conveyed authority to act coercively in such circumstances, then the second condition is also not met. Finally, because of the failure to establish a canonical ranking of social desiderata one will not be able to show whether a policy of tolerating euthanasia will lead to more benefits than harms. One will not know what ranking of values ought to be applied to assess the consequences.

This analysis is a backdoor introduction to the moral

equivalent of the legal notion of rights to privacy, areas where the state must show a compelling interest before it can constrain individual choice. Here the argument has been that where there is no clear justification for state authority, individuals are morally free to act. The right to euthanasia, like most other rights to act freely by oneself or with consenting others, is established negatively. It does not depend on some claim that such a liberty would be good, beneficial, or worth endorsing. Rather, it is a function of the failure to establish the authority of others, in particular, the state, to intervene coercively. With this, one comes face to face with the plausible limits of a secular state. Much must be tolerated because of the limits to the justifiable use of coercive state force. One is constrained to acquiesce in what is tantamount to a two-tier moral life: the first the world of moral understandings and intuitions that frame the concrete life of individuals when they meet as collaborators in a shared vision of the good life and the good death, and the second, the fabric of moral collaboration and negotiation that binds individuals together in peaceable joint endeavors when they meet as moral strangers. As a result, though one may deplore euthanasia because of one's beliefs as a Catholic, Orthodox Catholic, Jew, or Protestant (as do I), it is very likely not an act for which one can plausibly justify coercive state restraint in general secular terms.

One will need to live with individuals' deciding with consenting others when to end their lives, not because such is good, but because one does not have the authority coercively to stop individuals from acting together in such ways. In a secular, pluralist society one will need to accept euthanasia by default. One need not look to The Netherlands or elsewhere for models of what this might be like. In Texas up until 1973, neither suicide nor aiding and abetting suicide were criminalized. In articulating what was the old law in Texas, the Texas Supreme Court [in 1908] drew the line between what might be morally wrong and what the state would forbid:

It may be a violation of morals and ethics and reprehensible that a party may furnish another poison or pistols or guns or any other means or agency for the purpose of the suicide to take his own life, yet our law has not seen proper to punish such persons or such acts.

Like it or not, given the secular moral limitations of the authority of the state, we are all probably headed for Texas.

Part II

THROUGH DOCTORS' EYES

Most of the recent euthanasia debate has put doctors at the center of proposals to allow assisted suicide. Whether the emphasis on doctors' involvement is justified or not, it has obliged them to think seriously about their own position on the question. Here are two eloquent statements from the physicians' side.

Even his critics would tend to agree that Timothy Quill's "Death and Dignity: A Case of Individualized Decision Making" is the classic recent statement of a relatively responsible position on physician-assisted suicide. This does not mean that all who have considered Quill's position approve but only that, unlike in the "Debbie" scenario, the level of physician involvement is easier to defend. For example, Quill entertained his patient's request only after many encounters, after her psychological condition was assessed by a psychologist and he had conferred with her family; and (perhaps most important) he did not undertake the act himself but left that to his patient.

Unlike the "Debbie" scenario, this was a case of physician-assisted suicide, not active euthanasia. Still, as

Quill well knew, what he did was technically against the law, though even after his publication in the *New England Journal of Medicine*, he was not indicted for any crime. Perhaps our society has made an implicit decision not to introduce the law into morally treacherous territory. Or perhaps it is simply hesitant to try to decide about this issue at all.

Richard Selzer was, by his own account, far less certain of the rightness of the path a young man dying of AIDS asked him to take. On the contrary, he agonized over the decision even after he had made it. In this respect, he is perhaps like most of us, whether we are physicians or not.

Death and Dignity—A Case of Individualized Decision Making

Timothy E. Quill

Although Timothy Quill has been unalterably tied to this important article in the minds of many, before that he was a recognized authority on doctor-patient communication. He is a family physician and professor at the University of Rochester medical school. This paper appeared in the *New England Journal of Medicine* in 1991.

Diane was feeling tired and had a rash. A common scenario, though there was something subliminally worrisome that prompted me to check her blood count. Her hematocrit was 22, and the white-cell count was 4.3 with some metamyelocytes and unusual white cells. I wanted it to be viral, trying to deny what was staring me in the face. Perhaps in a repeated count it would disappear. I called Diane and told her it might be more serious than I had initially thought—that the test needed to be repeated and that if she felt worse, we might have to move quickly. When she pressed for the possibilities, I reluctantly opened the door to leukemia. Hearing the word seemed to make it exist. "Oh, shit!" she said. "Don't tell me that." Oh, shit! I thought. I wish I didn't have to.

Diane was no ordinary person (although no one I have ever come to know has been really ordinary). She was raised in an alcoholic family and had felt alone for much of her life. She had vaginal cancer as a young woman. Through much of her adult life, she had struggled with depression and her own alcoholism. I had come to know, respect, and admire her over the previous eight years as she confronted these problems and gradually overcame them. She was an incredibly clear, at times brutally honest, thinker and communicator. As she took control of her life, she developed a strong sense of independence and confidence. In the previous 3½ years, her hard work had paid off. She was completely abstinent from alcohol, she had established much deeper connections with her husband, college-age son, and several friends, and her business and her artistic work were blossoming. She felt she was really living fully for the first time.

Not surprisingly, the repeated blood count was abnormal, and detailed examination of the peripheral blood smear showed myelocytes. I advised her to come into the hospital, explaining that we needed to do a bone marrow biopsy and make some decisions relatively rapidly. She came to the hospital knowing what we would find. She was terrified, angry, and sad. Although we knew the odds, we both clung to the thread of possibility that it might be something else.

The bone marrow confirmed the worst: acute myelomonocytic leukemia. In the face of this tragedy, we looked for signs of hope. This is an area of medicine in which technological intervention has been successful, with cures 25 percent of the time—long-term cures. As I probed the costs of these cures, I heard about induction chemotherapy (three weeks in the hospital, prolonged neutropenia, probable infectious complications, and hair loss; 75 percent of patients respond, 25 percent do not). For the survivors, this is followed by consolidation chemotherapy (with similar side effects; another 25 percent die, for a net survival of 50 percent). Those still alive, to have a reasonable chance of long-term survival, then need bone marrow transplantation (hospitalization for two months and whole body irradiation, with complete killing of the bone marrow, infectious complications, and the possibility for graft-versus-host disease—with a survival of approximately 50 percent, or 25 percent of the original group). Though hematologists may argue over the exact percentages, they don't argue about the outcome of no treatment—certain death in days, weeks, or at most a few months.

Believing that delay was dangerous, our oncologist broke the news to Diane and began making plans to insert a Hickman catheter and begin induction chemotherapy that afternoon. When I saw her shortly thereafter, she was enraged at his presumption that she would want treatment, and devastated by the finality of the diagnosis. All she wanted to do was go home and be with her family. She had no further questions about treatment and in fact had decided that she wanted none. Together we lamented her tragedy and the unfairness of life. Before she left, I felt the need to be sure that she and her husband understood that there was some risk in delay, that the problem was not going to go away, and that we needed to keep considering the options over the next several days. We agreed to meet in two days.

She returned in two days with her husband and son. They had talked extensively about the problem and the options. She remained very clear about her wish not to undergo chemotherapy and to live whatever time she had left outside the hospital. As we explored her thinking further, it became clear that she was convinced she would die during the period of treatment and would suffer unspeakably in the process (from hospitalization, from lack of control over her body, from the side effects of chemotherapy, and from pain and anguish). Although I could offer support and my best effort to minimize her suffering if she chose treatment, there was no way I could say any of this would not occur. In fact, the last four patients with acute leukemia at our hospital had died very painful deaths in the hospital during various stages of treatment (a fact I did not share with her). Her family wished she would choose treatment but sadly accepted her decision. She articulated very clearly that it was she who would be experiencing all the side effects of treatment and that odds of 25 percent were not good enough for her to undergo so toxic a course of therapy, given her expectations of chemotherapy and hospitalization and the absence of a closely matched bone marrow donor. I had her repeat her understanding of the treatment, the odds, and what to expect if there were no treatment. I clarified a few misunderstandings, but she had a remarkable grasp of the options and implications.

I have been a longtime advocate of active, informed patient choice of treatment or nontreatment, and of a patient's right to die with as much control and dignity as possible. Yet there was something about her giving up a 25 percent chance of long-term survival in favor of almost certain death that disturbed me. I had seen Diane fight and use her considerable inner resources to overcome alcoholism and depression, and I half expected her to change her mind over the next week. Since the window of time in which effective treatment can be initiated is rather narrow, we met several times that week. We obtained a second hematology consultation and talked at length about the meaning and implications of treatment and nontreatment. She talked to a psychologist she had seen in the past. I gradually understood the decision from her perspective and became convinced that it was the right decision for her. We arranged for home hospice care (although at that time Diane felt reasonably well, was active, and looked healthy), left the door open for her to change her mind, and tried to anticipate how to keep her comfortable in the time she had left.

Just as I was adjusting to her decision, she opened up another area that would stretch me profoundly. It was extraordinarily important to Diane to maintain control of herself and her own dignity during the time remaining to her. When this was no longer possible, she clearly wanted to die. As a former director of a hospice program, I know how to use pain medicines to keep patients comfortable and lessen suffering. I explained the philosophy of comfort care, which I strongly believe in. Although Diane understood and appreciated this, she had known of people lingering in what was called relative comfort, and she wanted no part of it. When the time came, she wanted to take her life in the least painful way possible. Knowing of her desire for independence and her decision to stay in control, I thought this request made perfect sense. I acknowledged and explored this wish but also thought that it was out of the realm of currently accepted medical practice and that it was more than I could offer or promise. In our discussion, it became clear that preoccupation with her fear of a lingering death would interfere with Diane's getting the most out of the time she had left until she found a safe way to ensure her death. I feared the effects of a violent death on her family, the consequences of an ineffective suicide that would leave her lingering in precisely the state she dreaded so much, and the possibility that a family member would be forced to assist her, with all the legal and personal repercussions that would follow. She discussed this at length with her family. They believed that they should respect her choice. With this in mind, I told Diane that information was available from the Hemlock Society that might be helpful to her.

A week later she phoned me with a request for barbiturates for sleep. Since I knew that this was an essential ingredient in a Hemlock Society suicide, I asked her to come to the office to talk things over. She was more than willing to protect me by participating in a superficial conversation about her insomnia, but it was important to me to know how she planned to use the drugs and to be sure that she was not in despair or overwhelmed in a way that might color her judgment. In our discussion, it was apparent that she was having trouble sleeping, but it was also evident that the security of having enough barbiturates available to commit suicide when and if the time came would leave her secure enough to live fully and concentrate on the present. It was clear that she was not despondent and that in fact she was making deep, personal connections with her family and close friends. I made sure that she knew how to use the barbiturates for sleep, and also that she knew the amount needed to commit suicide. We agreed to meet regularly, and she promised to meet with me before taking her life, to ensure that all other avenues had been exhausted. I wrote the prescription with an uneasy feeling about the boundaries I was exploring—spiritual, legal, professional, and personal. Yet I also felt strongly that I was setting her free to get the most out of the time she had left, and to maintain dignity and control on her own terms until her death.

The next several months were very intense and important for Diane. Her son stayed home from college and they were able to be with one another and say much that had not been said earlier. Her husband did his work at home so that he and Diane could spend more time together. She spent time with her closest friends. I had her come into the hospital for a conference with our residents, at which she illustrated in a most profound and personal way the importance of informed decision making, the right to refuse treatment, and the extraordinarily personal effects of illness and interaction with the medical system. There were emotional and physical hardships as well. She had periods of intense sadness and anger. Several times she became very weak, but she received transfusions as an outpatient and responded with marked improvement of symptoms. She had two serious infections that responded surprisingly well to empirical courses of oral antibiotics. After three tumultuous months, there were two weeks of relative calm and well-being, and fantasies of a miracle began to surface.

Unfortunately, we had no miracle. Bone pain, weakness, fatigue, and fevers began to dominate her life. Although the hospice workers, family members, and I tried our best to minimize the suffering and promote comfort, it was clear that the end was approaching. Diane's immediate future held what she feared the most—increasing discomfort, dependence, and hard choices between pain and sedation. She called up her closest friends and asked them to come over to say goodbye, telling them that she would be leaving soon. As we had agreed, she let me know as well. When we met, it was clear that she knew what she was doing, that she was sad and frightened to be leaving, but that she would be even more terrified to stay and suffer. In our tearful goodbye, she promised a reunion in the future at her favorite spot on the edge of Lake Geneva, with dragons swimming in the sunset.

Two days later her husband called to say that Diane had died. She had said her final goodbyes to her husband and son that morning, and asked them to leave her alone for an hour. After an hour, which must have seemed an eternity, they found her on the couch, lying very still and covered by her favorite shawl. There was no sign of struggle. She seemed to be at peace. They called me for advice about how to proceed. When I arrived at their house, Diane indeed seemed peaceful. Her husband and son were quiet. We talked about what a remarkable person she had been. They seemed to have no doubts about the course she had chosen or about their cooperation, although the unfairness of her illness and the finality of her death were overwhelming to us all.

I called the medical examiner to inform him that a hospice patient had died. When asked about the cause of death, I said, "acute leukemia." He said that was fine and that we should call a funeral director. Although acute leukemia was the truth, it was not the whole story. Yet any mention of suicide would have given rise to a police investigation and probably brought the arrival of an ambulance crew for resuscitation. Diane would have become a "coroner's case," and the decision to perform an autopsy would have been made at the discretion of the medical examiner. The family or I could have been subject to criminal prosecution, and I to professional review, for our roles in support of Diane's choices. Although I truly believe that the family and I gave her the best care possible, allowing her to define her limits and directions as much as possible, I am not sure the law, society, or the medical profession would agree. So I said "acute leukemia" to protect all of us, to protect Diane from an invasion into her past and her body, and to continue to shield society from the knowledge of the degree of suffering that people often undergo in the process of dying. Suffering can be lessened to some extent, but in no way eliminated or made benign, by the careful intervention of a competent, caring physician, given current social constraints.

Diane taught me about the range of help I can provide if

I know people well and if I allow them to say what they really want. She taught me about life, death, and honesty and about taking charge and facing tragedy squarely when it strikes. She taught me that I can take small risks for people that I really know and care about. Although I did not assist in her suicide directly, I helped indirectly to make it possible, successful, and relatively painless. Although I know we have measures to help control pain and lessen suffering, to think that people do not suffer in the process of dying is an illusion. Prolonged dying can occasionally be peaceful, but more often the role of the physician and family is limited to lessening but not eliminating severe suffering.

I wonder how many families and physicians secretly help patients over the edge into death in the face of such severe suffering. I wonder how many severely ill or dying patients secretly take their lives, dying alone in despair. I wonder whether the image of Diane's final aloneness will persist in the minds of her family, or if they will remember more the intense, meaningful months they had together before she died. I wonder whether Diane struggled in that last hour, and whether the Hemlock Society's way of death by suicide is the most benign. I wonder why Diane, who gave so much to so many of us, had to be alone for the last hour of her life. I wonder whether I will see Diane again, on the shore of Lake Geneva at sunset, with dragons swimming on the horizon.

A Question of Mercy

Richard Selzer

Richard Selzer, who is a professor of medicine at Yale University, is part of a distinguished tradition of physicians who have mastered the literary expression of their professional experience. This piece was first published in the *New York Times Magazine* in September 1991.

Almost two years ago, I received a phone call from a poet I knew slightly. Would I, he wondered, be willing to intervene on behalf of a friend of his who was dying of AIDS?

"Intervene?"

"His suffering is worthy of Job. He wants to commit suicide while he still has the strength to do it."

"Do you know what you're asking?"

"I know, I know."

"No," I told him. "I'm trained to preserve life, not end it. It's not in me to do a thing like that."

"Are you saying that a doctor should prolong a misfortune as long as possible?"

"There is society," I replied. "There is the law. I'm not a barbarian."

"You are precisely that," he said. "A barbarian."

His accusation reminded me of an incident in the life of Ambroise Paré the father of surgery, who in the 16th century accompanied the armies of France on their campaigns. Once, on entering a newly captured city, Paré looked for a barn in which to keep his horse while he treated the wounded. Inside he found four dead soldiers and three more still alive, their faces contorted with pain, their clothes still smoldering where the gunpowder had burned them.

As Paré gazed at the wounded with pity, an old soldier came up and asked whether there was any way to cure them. Paré shook his head, whereupon the old soldier went

63

up to the men and, Paré recounted in his memoirs, cut their throats "gently, efficiently and without ill will." Horrified at what he thought a great cruelty, Paré cried out to the executioner that he was a villain.

"No," said the man. "I pray to God that if ever I come to be in that condition, someone will do the same for me." Was this an act of villainy, or mercy?

The question still resists answering. Last year, a Michigan court heard the case of a doctor who supplied a woman with his "suicide machine"—a simple apparatus that allows a patient to self-administer a lethal dose of drugs intravenously. Since then, it seems that each day brings reports of deaths assisted by doctors. A best-selling book, "Final Exit," written by the director of the Hemlock Society, now instructs us in painless ways to commit suicide should the dreadful occasion arise. Even the most ideologically opposed must now hear the outcry of a populace for whom the dignity and mercy of a quick pharmacological death may be preferable to a protracted, messy and painful end.

"But why are you calling *me?*" I asked my friend.

"I've read your books. It occurred to me that you might just be the right one."

I let the poet know that I had retired from medicine five years before, that I was no longer a doctor.

"Once a doctor, always a doctor," he replied.

What I did not tell him was that each year I have continued to renew the license that allows me to prescribe narcotics. You never know. . . . Some day I might have need of them to relieve pain or to kill myself easily should the occasion arise. If for myself, then why not for another?

"I'll think about it," I said. He gave me the address and phone number.

"I implore you," said the poet.

The conversation shifted to the abominable gymnastics of writing, a little gossip. We hung up.

Don't, I told myself.

Diary. Jan. 14, 1990

My friend's friend lives with a companion on the seventh floor of an apartment building about a 10-minute walk from my house. The doorman on duty is a former patient of mine. He greets me warmly, lifts his shirt to show me his gallbladder incision, how well it has healed.

"You can hardly see it," he says. That is the sort of thing that happens when I leave my study and re-enter the world. The doorman buzzes me in.

At precisely 4 P.M., as arranged, I knock on the apartment door. It is opened by L., a handsome, perhaps too handsome, man in his late 30's. We recognized each other's presence on the Yale campus. He is an ordained minister. He tells me that he has made use of my writings in his sermons. In the living room, R. is sitting on an invalid's cushion on the sofa. A short, delicate man, also in his 30's, R. is a doctor specializing in public health—women's problems, birth control, family planning, AIDS. He is surprisingly unwasted, although pale as a blank sheet of paper. He gives me a brilliant smile around even white teeth. The eyes do not participate in the smile. L. and R. have been lovers for six years.

R.'s hair is close-cropped, black; there is a neat lawn of beard. He makes a gesture as if to stand, but I stop him. His handshake is warm and dry and strong. There is a plate of chocolate chip cookies on a table. L. pours tea. L.'s speech is clipped, slightly mannered. R. has a Hispanic accent; he is Colombian.

For a few minutes we step warily around the reason I have come. Then, all at once, we are engaged. I ask R. about his symptoms. He tells me of his profound fatigue, the depression, the intractable diarrhea, his ulcerated hemorrhoids. He has Kaposi's sarcoma. Only yesterday a new lesion appeared in the left naso-orbital region, the area between the nose and eye. He points to it. Through his beard I see another large black tumor. His mouth is dry, encrusted from the dehydration that comes with chronic diarrhea. Now and then he clutches his abdomen, grimaces. There is the odor of stool.

"I want to die," he announces calmly.

"Is it so bad?"

"Yes, it is."

"But how can I be sure? On Tuesday, you want to die; by Thursday, perhaps you will have changed your mind."

He nods to L., who helps him to stand. The three of us go into their bedroom, where R., lying on his side, offers his lesions as evidence. I see that his anus is a great circular ulceration, raw and oozing blood. His buttocks are smeared with pus and liquid stool. With tenderness, L. bathes and dresses him in a fresh diaper. Even though I have been summoned here, I feel very much the intruder upon their privacy. And I am convinced.

We return to the living room. L. and R. sit side by side on the sofa, holding hands. A lethal dose of barbiturates is being mailed by a doctor friend in Colombia. R. wants to be certain that it will not fail, that someone will be on hand to administer a final, fatal dose if he should turn out to be physically too weak to take the required number of pills. He also wants L. to be with him, holding him. He asks that L. not cry. He couldn't bear that, he says. L. says that of course he will cry, that he must be allowed to. L. is afraid, too, that it might not work, that he will be discovered as an accomplice.

"I am the sole beneficiary of the will," he explains. L. does not want to be alone when the time comes. He has never seen anyone die before. (A minister? Has he never attended a deathbed?) "It has just worked out that way," he says, as though reading my mind. Still, I am shocked at such a state of virginity.

We have a discussion. It is about death as best friend, not enemy. How sensible were the pagans, for whom death was a return to the spirit world that resides in nature. One member of the tribe vanishes forever, but the tribe itself lives on. It is a far cry from the Christian concept of death and resurrection.

R. passes a hand across his eyes as if to brush away a veil. His vision is failing; soon he will be blind. He coughs, shifts on the pillow, swallows a pain pill. He tells me that he has taken all of the various experimental medicines without relief of the diarrhea. His entire day is spent medicating himself and dealing with the incontinence. Despite chemotherapy, the tumors are growing rapidly. His palate is covered with them. He opens his mouth for me to see. Above all, he wants to retain his dignity, to keep control of his life, which he equates with choosing the time and method of suicide. Soon he will be unable to do it.

"But death," I say. "It's so final."

"I want it," he says again, on his face a look of longing. He wants me to promise that I will obtain the additional narcotics that would insure death, if needed. I offer only to return in a few days to talk. R. urges me to think of myself as an instrument that he himself will use for his rescue. An instrument? But I am a man.

The tone turns conspiratorial. Our voices drop. We admonish each other to be secretive, tell no one. There are those who would leap to punish. I suggest that R. arrange for a codicil to his will requesting that there be no autopsy.

Jan. 16

Four in the afternoon. R. answers the door. He has lost ground. His eyes are sunken, his gait tottering. He is in great pain, which he makes no effort to conceal. As arranged, he is alone. L. is to return in an hour. The barbiturates have arrived from Colombia. He shows me the bottles of tablets in the bottom drawer of the dresser. A quick calculation tells me that he has well over the lethal dose. The diarrhea has been unrelenting. The Kaposi's sarcoma is fulminating, with new lesions every day.

"I have always counted so much on my looks," he says shyly and without the least immodesty. "And now I have become something that no one would want to touch." Without a pause, he asks, "What if I vomit the pills?" I tell him to take them at a regular pace, each with only a sip of water so as not to fill up too quickly. If necessary, would I inject more medication? "I have good veins," he says, and rolls up a sleeve. I see that he does. There are several needle puncture marks at the antecubital fossa—the front of the elbow—where blood has been drawn. One more would not be noticed.

"When?" I ask him. No later than one month from today. Do I want to choose a date? R. rises with difficulty, gets a calendar from the kitchen. We bend over it.

"Are you free on Feb. 10?" he asks. "It's a Saturday."

"I'm free."

Feb. 10! There is a date!

I ask R. about his life. He was born and raised in Medellín, one of four sisters and three brothers. His mother had no formal education, but she is "very wise." It is clear that he loves her. No, she knows nothing; neither that he is gay nor that he is ill. He has written a letter to be sent after his death, telling her that he loves her, thanking her for all that she has done. In the family, only an older brother knows that he is gay, and to him it is a disgrace. He has forbidden R. to tell the others. His sisters live near his mother in Medellín. There are 12 grandchildren. She will not be alone. (He smiles at this.)

Had he always known he was gay? He discovered his attraction to men at age 8, but of course it was impossible to express it. Colombia is intolerant of homosexuality. At 17, he went to Bogotá to study medicine. For six years he lived in an apartment with four other students. There was close camaraderie but no sexual expression. It was a "quiet" student's life. After one year of internship in a hospital, he decided against clinical medicine.

It was while working toward a degree in public health at Yale that he met L. The year was 1983. After completing his studies, he was separated from L. for two years, working in another city, although he returned to visit L. frequently. There followed a three-year period when they lived together in New Haven. Shortly after they met, R. began to feel ill, thought he had an infection. He suspected it was AIDS. He told L. at once and they agreed to discontinue sex. Aside from mutual caressing, there has been no sexual contact between them since.

"It was not sex that brought us together," he says. "It was love." I lower my gaze, I who have always hesitated before expressing love.

L. returns. It is the first day of the semester at Yale. A day of meeting with students, advising, counseling. He is impeccably dressed. He is accompanied by a woman, someone I know slightly. He notices my surprise.

"This is M.," he announces. "She's all right." He places his arm around her waist, explaining that they have been close friends and confidantes for many years. "She is the sister I have always wanted." L. bends to kiss R. on the cheek.

"*Chiquito!* You are wearing your new shirt," says L. I am alarmed by the presence of M. It is clear that she knows everything. We sit around the table drinking tea.

"Tell me about death," said L.

"What do you mean?"

"The details. You're a doctor, you should know. What about the death rattle?"

"It has been called that." I explain about not being able to clear secretions from the lungs.

"What sort of equipment will we need?"

"Nothing. You already have the diapers."

"R. has to die in diapers?" I explain about the relaxation of the bowel and urinary sphincters, that it would be best.

"I shouldn't have asked." L. seems increasingly nervous. "I'm terrified of the police," he says. "I always have been. Should I see a lawyer? What if I'm caught and put in prison?" He begins to weep openly. "And I'm losing R. That is a fact, and there is not a thing I can do about it!" When he continues to cry without covering his face, R. reaches out a hand to console him.

"Look," I say. "You're not ready for this and, to tell the truth, I'm not sure I am either."

"Oh please!" R.'s voice is a high-pitched whine of distress. "It is only a matter of a few minutes of misery. I would be dying anyway after that."

L. pulls himself together, nods to show that he understands. I begin to feel that my presence is putting pressure on him; it makes R.'s death real, imminent. I tell him that I am ready to withdraw. How easy that would be. A way out.

"You are the answer to R.'s prayers," he says. "To him you are an angel." But to L. I am the angel of death. "Of course, I agree to whatever R. wants to do," he says. It is R. who turns practical.

"If it is too hard for you, L., I won't mind if you are not here with me." And to me: "L. simply cannot lie. If questioned by the police, he would have to tell the truth." I see that the lying will be up to me. All the while, M. has remained silent.

We go through the "script"—L.'s word. In the bedroom, R. will begin taking pills. I will help him. L. and M. will wait in the living room.

L.:   "Will we be in the apartment all the time until he dies?"

M. (speaking for the first time):
       "Not necessary. We can go out somewhere and return to find him dead."

L.:   "Where would we go?"

M.:   "Anywhere. For a walk; to the movies."

L.:   "How long will it take?"

Me: "Perhaps all day."

L.:   "What if the doctors notify the police? R. has made no secret of his intention at the clinic. They have even withheld pain medication because he is 'high risk.'"

Me (to R.):
   "Next time you go the clinic, ask for a
   prescription for 50 Levo-Dromoran
   tablets. It's a narcotic. Maybe they'll give
   you that many. Maybe not."

L.:   "I simply can't believe they would turn
   us in, but there's no way to be sure, is
   there?"

More and more we are like criminals, or a cell of revo-
lutionaries. L.'s fear and guilt are infectious. But then there
is R. I stand up to leave, assuring them that I will come
again on Sunday at 4 in the afternoon. M. says that she will
be there, too. L. hopes he has not shaken my resolve. He
apologizes for his weakness.
   "We'll talk further," I say. R. takes my hand. "You have
become my friend. In such a short time. One of the best
friends of my life."

Jan. 17

In the mail there is a note from L. in his small, neat
handwriting. He thanks me. Enclosed is a copy of a lec-
ture he had given in 1984 in which he cited an incident
from one of my books, about a doctor who, entreated by
a suffering patient who wants to die, stays his hand out of
mercy. It is strangely prophetic and appropriate to the
circumstances.
   My nights are ridden with visions: I am in the bedroom
with R. We are sitting side by side on the bed. He is wearing
only a large blue disposable diaper. The bottles of pills are
on the night stand along with a pitcher of water and a glass.
R. pours a handful of the tiny tablets into his palm, then
with a shy smile begins to swallow them one at a time.
Because of the dryness of his mouth and the fungal infection of his throat, it is painful. And slow.

"You're drinking too much water," I say. "You'll fill up too quickly."

"I will try," he says. What seems like hours go by. From the living room comes the sound of Mozart's Clarinet Quintet. R. labors on, panting, coughing. When he has finished one bottle, I open another. His head and arms begin to wobble. I help him to lie down.

"Quickly," I tell him. "We don't have much time left." I hold the glass for him, guide it to his lips. He coughs, spits out the pills.

"Hold me," he says. I bend above him, cradle his head in my arm.

"Let yourself go," I say. He does, and minutes later he is asleep. I free myself and count the pills that are left, calculate the milligrams. Not enough. It is too far below the lethal dose. I take a vial of morphine and a syringe from a pocket, a rubber tourniquet. I draw up 10 cc. of the fluid and inject it into a vein in R.'s arm. The respirations slow down at once. I palpate his pulse. It wavers, falters, stops. There is a long last sigh from the pillow.

All at once, a key turns in the door to the hallway. The door is flung open. Two men in fedoras and raincoats enter the bedroom. They are followed by the doorman whose gallbladder I had removed.

"You are under arrest," one of them announces.

"What is the charge?" I ask, clinging to a pretense of innocence. "For the murder of R.C." I am startled by the mention of his last name. Had I known it? I am led away.

Jan. 21

M., L., R. and I: R.'s smile of welcome plays havoc with my heart. It is easy to see why L. fell in love with him. I offer an alternative: R. could simply stop eating and drinking. It would not take too many days. Neither L. nor R. can accept this. L. cannot watch R. die of thirst. There is a new black tumor on R.'s upper lip. He has visited the clinic and ob-

tained 30 Levo-Dromoran tablets. Suddenly, I feel I must
test him again.

Me: "I don't think you're ready. Feb. 10 is
        too soon."

R. (covering his face with his hands,
moaning):
        "Why do you say that?"

Me: "Because you haven't done it already.
        Because you've chosen a method that is
        not certain. Because you're worrying
        about L."

L.:   "I feel that I'm an obstruction."

Me: "No, but you're unreliable. You cannot
        tell the lies that may be necessary."

L.:   "I'm sorry, I'm sorry."

Me: "Don't apologize for virtue. It doesn't
        make sense."

R.:   "There is one thing. I prefer to do it at
        night, after dark. It would be easier for
        me."

That, if nothing else, is comprehensible. Youth bids farewell to the moon more readily than to the sun.

We rehearse the revised plan. L., M. and R. will dine
together, "love each other," say goodbye. L. and M. will
take the train to New York for the night. At 6 P.M. R. will
begin to take the pills. At 8:30 I will let myself into the
apartment. The doorman may or may not question me, but
I will have a key. I will stay only long enough to be sure that
R. is dead. If he is not, I will use the morphine; if he is, I will
not notify anyone. At noon the next day, L. and M. will
return to discover the body and call the clinic. It is most
likely that a doctor will come to pronounce death. Of

course, he will ask questions, perhaps notice something, demand an autopsy. In that case, L. will show him the codicil to the will. M. asks whether the codicil is binding. At the end of the session we are all visibly exhausted.

Feb. 3

Our final visit. R. is worried that because of the diarrhea he will not absorb the barbiturate. He has seen undigested potassium tables in his stool. I tell him not to worry; I will make sure. His gratitude is infinitely touching, infinitely sad. We count the pills. There are 110 of them, totaling 11 grams. The lethal dose is 4.5. He also had the remaining Levo-Dromoran tablets. I have already obtained the vial of morphine and the syringe. R. is bent, tormented, but smiles when I hug him goodbye.

"I'll see you on Saturday," I tell him.

"But I won't see you," he replies with a shy smile. On the elevator, I utter aloud a prayer that I will not have to use the morphine.

Feb. 7

Lunch at a restaurant with L. and M.

"It's no good," M. says to me. "You're going to get caught."

"What makes you think so?"

"Why would a doctor with a practice of one patient be present at his death, especially when the patient is known to be thinking about suicide?" She has contacted the Hemlock Society and talked with a sympathetic lawyer. She was told that there is no way to prevent an autopsy. By Connecticut law, the newly dead must be held for 48 hours before cremation, R.'s preference. The coroner will see the body. Because of R.'s youth and the suspicion of suicide, the coroner will order an autopsy. Any injected substance would be discovered. The time of death can be estimated with some accuracy. I would have been seen entering the building around that time. The police would ask questions. Interviewed separately, L., M. and I would give conflicting answers. I would be named. There would be the publicity, the press. It would be vicious. "No, you're fired, and that's that." I long to give in to the wave of relief that seeps over me. But there is R.

"What about R. and my promise?"

"We just won't tell him that you're not coming."

"The coward's way," I say.

"That's what we are, aren't we?"

Feb. 11

A phone call from L.: R. is "very much alive." He is at the hospital, in the intensive-care unit. They have put him on a respirator, washed out his stomach. He is being fed intravenously.

"I had to call the ambulance, didn't I?" he asks. "What else could I do? He was alive."

Feb. 15

The intensive-care unit is like a concrete blockhouse. The sound of 20 respirators, each inhaling and exhaling at its own pace, makes a steady wet noise like the cascade from a fountain. But within minutes of one's arrival, it becomes interwoven with the larger fabric of sound—the clatter and thump, the quick footfalls, the calling out, the moaning. Absolute silence would be louder.

From the doorway I observe the poverty of R.'s body, the way he shivers like a wet dog. The draining away of his flesh and blood is palpable. The skin of his hands is as chaste and dry, as beautiful as old paper. I picture him as a small bird perched on an arrow that has been shot and is flying somewhere.

"R.!" I call out. He opens his eyes and looks up, on his face a look that I can only interpret as reproach or disappointment. He knows that I was not there. L. the Honest has told him.

"Do you want to be treated for the pneumonia?" I ask. He cannot speak for the tube in his trachea, but he nods. "Do you want to live?" R. nods again. "Do you still want to die?" R. shakes his head no.

Twelve days later, R. died in the hospital. Three days after that, I met L. on the street. We were shy, embarrassed, like two people who share a shameful secret.

"We must get together soon," said L.

"By all means. We should talk." We never did.

Part III

THE DUTCH MODEL

This part begins with a dramatic transcript of a case of active euthanasia, as practiced in the Netherlands. As Margaret Pabst Battin explains, euthanasia and physician-assisted suicide have a quasilegal status in the Netherlands. Although this has been the case for some time, relatively little reliable data has been available concerning the way this policy of toleration has worked. What does seem clear is that the practice has been largely underreported and that, to satisfy the judicial guidelines, a physician must devote considerably more time and care to the act than that exhibited by the resident in the "Debbie" scenario. Even among those who are sympathetic to the Dutch model, few regard the actions in "Debbie" as remotely acceptable. Their example of the Dutch model in America is more likely to be something like Timothy Quill's management of his patient.

Nat Hentoff is concerned mainly with the gradual loss of respect for life that could be engendered by a widespread toleration of euthanasia or assisted suicide. The immediate context for his comments was the November 1992 ballot initiative in California that would have legalized active, voluntary euthanasia for terminally ill patients in that state. The California referendum was the second of its kind, the first being in Washington State and the third in Oregon, which passed in 1994. Hentoff's piece anticipates the next part of the book, in which we examine closely these other two ballot initiatives. If Hentoff is right, then the Oregon Trail will turn out to be a slippery slope.

Guy I. Benrubi responds to the slippery-slope worry partly by appealing to the lessons of the Dutch model. He proposes some important additions, however, including a new physician specialty, specific training in the painless termination of life. This approach seems unlikely to quiet the fears of those like Hentoff, but Benrubi situates the debate in clinical reality.

Helping a Man Kill Himself, as Shown on Dutch TV

Tom Kuntz

These excerpts from a Dutch television documentary on active euthanasia were published in the *New York Times* on November 13, 1994, with an introduction by Tom Kuntz.

The movement in the United States to allow mercy killing—Dr. Jack Kevorkian is its most controversial exponent—reached a milestone last week when voters in Oregon approved the nation's first law allowing doctors to hasten death for the terminally ill.

The law takes effect Dec. 8, and doctors following its guidelines cannot be prosecuted if they prescribe a lethal dose of drugs to terminally ill patients who request it. At least two doctors must first agree that the patient has six months or less to live and the patient must ask three times, the last time in writing. Doctors have to wait 15 days before meeting the final request for a lethal prescription.

Such conditions echo some of those in the euthanasia law enacted late last year in the Netherlands, a nation at the vanguard of mercy killing. Euthanasia remains illegal in Holland, but it is not prosecuted if the law's strictures are met.

The Dutch process was vividly illustrated on Oct. 20, when the Netherlands achieved another milestone: the first national broadcast of an actual mercy killing. Scenes and dialogue from the somber and wrenching documentary "Death on Request" are excerpted here, from a videotape with English subtitles provided by Ikon, the Dutch TV network that produced it. Ikon says the documentary has not yet been licensed for distribution in English.

The hour-long documentary by Maarten Nederhorst follows a terminally ill former Amsterdam restaurateur, Cornelis van Wendel de Joode, 63, his wife, Antoinette, and Mr. van Wendel's physician, Wilfred van Oijen, from December through the patient's death in March. Mr. van Wendel—referred to by his nickname Kees—is suffering from amyotrophic lateral sclerosis (Lou Gehrig's disease), an incurable, degenerative neurological condition. The physician arrives at the riverside Amsterdam apartment of Kees and Antoinette.

> Wife (interpreting for husband, who is able
> only to mumble as a result of his
> condition): He doesn't want to go to
> hospital. And no artificial respiration
> either. He'd be a vegetable. . . .

> Doctor:
> You say that you want to make your own
> decision, meaning: I want to decide
> myself when I want to stop living.

> Kees: Yeah . . . We mustn't wait any
> longer. . . .

> Doctor:
> I suggest that in any case we should
> consult a second doctor so he can still
> talk to you as I am doing now. It may
> not be possible in three weeks.

> Kees: It will be necessary to ask a second
> doctor to come now. We mustn't
> wait. . . .

> Doctor:
> No—You are upset, Kees, aren't you?
> (Cut to patient weeping.)

> Doctor:
> Come, here's a handkerchief. There,
> there. Take my handkerchief. . . .

Wife: Let's change the subject. Otherwise he
    won't stop.

Doctor:
    No, it's all right. Wait. It's
    understandable. It's the most essential
    decision he'll ever take. . . .

On a later day, a second doctor (unidentified) arrives at
the couple's apartment. Kees is now shown with a letter
board on his lap, on which he can spell out words.

Second doctor:
    Perhaps you'd like to know why I am
    here. It's necessary if we are to carry
    out euthanasia legally you have to sat-
    isfy a number of conditions. Those are:
    hopeless suffering with no prospect of a
    cure; and repeated requests for euthana-
    sia, when you feel further life is unac-
    ceptable. In your case most of these
    conditions apply. You have an incurable
    disease which will soon end in death
    and unless there is some intervention
    you will experience terrible suffering.
    You'll probably suffocate.

Kees: Yes (points to letter board, and laughs
    sardonically, evidently at the fact that he
    is now legally qualified to die).

Wife: Passed the test. Yes, he has passed the
    test.

Doctor:
    Yes, he has passed the test. . . .

The first doctor, Dr. van Oijen, is shown in his office on
the phone with the neurologist.

Doctor:

Any ideas about medication? Usually I
give a sedative, phenobarbital or suchlike,
intramuscular, and when he's well under
I shall use a curare-type thing.

Neurologist:

There are few alternatives in the case of
Mr. van Wendel because he wants to die
at home.

At his house, Dr. van Oijen is shown seated at a table.

Interviewer:

What about one of the Ten
Commandments, "Thou shalt not kill?"

Doctor:

Well, I have no plans to mow down a
number of people with my Uzi. So, in
that sense, killing is the worst thing I can
imagine. But that's entirely different from
when I as a doctor care for people and
insure they don't suffer unnecessarily. . . .
That's quite different.

Interviewer:

Is it so that when you tell people you'll
help them at the end that they tend to
live longer?

Doctor:

Yes, I'm sure of that. . . . What I
experience regularly is that although
euthanasia has been arranged it's not
carried out, that a person fights on until
the last. . . . But I think they have then
lived longer because they could ask for
help if needed.

It is the evening of March 3, Kees's 63d birthday—the day on which he has chosen to die. The doctor arrives at the apartment, dressed casually.

> Kees (to doctor):
>> Is it rough for you too?
>
> Doctor:
>> Well, my feet were dragging a bit on the way here. (Both laugh nervously.)
>
> Doctor:
>> But should we wait much longer, Kees, or do you think—
>
> Wife: Let him finish his port.
>
> Doctor:
>> Oh, of course. . . . (Kees is able to sip his wine clumsily through a straw.)
>
> Wife: Your health—is that what you're saying?
>
> Kees (toasting doctor):
>> Your health.
>
> Doctor:
>> Thank you.
>
> Wife (reading what Kees spells out on the letter board):
>> Let . . . us . . . post . . . pone . . . not . . . any . . . longer. Let's go.
>
> Doctor:
>> If you wish, Kees, we could do it tomorrow . . . (But Kees turns his wheelchair and heads into the next room toward his hospital bed.)

His wife dresses him for bed as the doctor fills a syringe. A closeup shows him giving Kees an injection in the left arm.

Doctor:
>This is just for falling asleep. The idea is
>that you'll doze off nicely now. You
>won't have any dreams but you'll sleep
>well. It has to go through the
>bloodstream, so it could take 5 or 10
>minutes. . . . (smiling at patient) This is
>right, eh, Kees? (To wife) Is it distressing
>for you to see him now?

Wife: No . . .

Doctor:
>Quite beautiful.

Wife: Very peaceful, yes. It's strange to think
that it'll stop. He's so quiet, so relaxed.

Doctor:
>He certainly is. I'll prepare the other
>injection, right?

(Wife kisses husband a last time.)

Doctor:
>Now he's deep down, isn't he?

Wife: Yes, I think so. . . . I was saying, we're
doing it together . . . like we always did
. . . only I can't come along now (she
weeps). You have to go out on your own.
. . .

   The doctor administers what is apparently the final lethal
injection (an Ikon spokesman said three injections were
used in Kees's euthanasia, yet only two are shown).

Doctor:
>You can see him going.

Wife: Look here . . . less heart . . . It's all over
at last. Finally it's all over. . . .

The wife holds Kees's arm, the doctor behind her with his arm around her. There is a wake-like interval. The doctor reads a final letter by Kees to his wife. The city coroner is notified—a man in spectacles.

Coroner:
It all goes to the public prosecutor.

Doctor:
It's a strange idea really, that a non-medical person's going to sit in judgment.

Coroner:
That's the procedure. It's for the Ministry of Justice. I'll ring the public prosecutor from here, right now. . . . And then he'll take a decision on whether to clear the body for burial. . . .

Coroner (speaking on the phone):
I'm the police doctor on duty, and I wish to report a case of euthanasia. . . .

A Dozen Caveats Concerning the Discussion of Euthanasia in the Netherlands

Margaret Pabst Battin

Margaret Pabst Battin is a professor of philosophy at the University of Utah who has followed the euthanasia and assisted-suicide discussion for some time, with special attention to the situation in Holland. This paper was part of her 1994 anthology called *The Least Worst Death*.

A s the discussion of voluntary active euthanasia heats up in the United States, increasing attention is being given to its practice in the Netherlands. There, euthanasia (and with it, physician-assisted suicide) is more and more openly discussed and practiced; it is performed with the knowledge of the legal authorities; physicians who follow the guidelines are protected from prosecution; and, as a result of broad public discussions of the issue in the media, euthanasia is familiar to virtually all Dutch residents as an option in end-of-life medical care.

In the United States, those who think euthanasia should be legalized often cite the Netherlands as a model of conscientious practice; those who think it should not be legalized, on the other hand, often claim that Dutch practice already involves abuse and will inevitably lead to more. For the most part, these generalizations invite misunderstanding, and they often reflect only the antecedent biases of those who make them. I would like to offer a few caveats for those about to become embroiled in the discussion of euthanasia, as the United States debates whether it, too, will permit this practice—caveats offered in the hope of contributing to better mutual understanding rather than greater polarization over this extremely volatile issue.

I. Legal Claims Are Misleading, Either Way

Many American observers of the Dutch practice of euthanasia are tempted to claim that euthanasia is legal in Holland; others insist that it is not. Both are right—but only partly so. Killing at the request of the person killed as well as assistance in suicide remain crimes under the Dutch penal code, punishable by imprisonment; however, lower and supreme court decisions, reflected in the policies of the regional attorneys-general, further promulgated by the Royal Dutch Medical Association, have held that when euthanasia is performed in accord with a set of guidelines it may be defended under a plea of *force majeure* and so is reasonably sure of not being prosecuted. Recent legal changes have revised the earlier requirement that a physician report euthanasia he or she performs directly to the police; now, under a policy intended to encourage far more self-reporting, the physician is expected to describe the circumstances surrounding and the reasons for euthanasia to the coroner, who is to confer with the local prosecutor and if satisfied that the case meets the guidelines, will issue a certificate of no objection to burial or cremation of the body; the case is not further prosecuted.

The guidelines, incorporated into statute June 1, 1994, are called "rules of due care." They are questions the physician is expected to answer in reflecting on whether his or her action in providing euthanasia has been appropriate. Recent cases, including highly visible cases concerning euthanasia provided at her request to an intractably depressed woman and euthanasia for a newborn with spina bifida and hydrocephalus, are currently serving to define the limits of the Dutch practice, but the broad Dutch consensus favoring euthanasia concerns only voluntary choice by a competent patient. The guidelines, roughy divided into two groups, can be stated as follows:

SUBSTANTIVE GUIDELINES

(a)   Euthanasia must be voluntary; the patient's request must be seriously considered and enduring.

(b)   The patient must have adequate information about his or her medical condition, the prognosis, and alternative methods of treatment.

(c)   The patient's suffering must be intolerable, in the patient's view, and irreversible (though it is not required that the patient be terminally ill).

(d)   It must be the case that there are no reasonable alternatives for relieving the patient's suffering that are acceptable to the patient.

PROCEDURAL GUIDELINES

(e)   Euthanasia may be performed only by a physician (though a nurse may assist the physician).

(f)   The physician must consult with a second physician whose judgment can be expected to be independent.

(g)   The physician must exercise due care in reviewing and verifying the patient's condition as well as in performing the euthanasia procedure itself.

(h)   The relatives must be informed unless the patient does not wish this.

(i)   There should be a written record of the case.

(j)   The case may not be reported as a natural death.

Is euthanasia legal or illegal? It is a violation of the statute but is *gedoogd* or "tolerated" if it meets these guidelines, and will not be prosecuted. Yet it is not excused in advance, and the plea of *force majeure*, although often compelling in single cases, does not easily serve as a basis for policy. Until 1990, it was required that any case of euthanasia be reported to the police and investigated after the fact, further prosecution being set aside if the case met the guidelines; in fact, comparatively few cases were reported, and physicians complained that they—and patients' families—were being treated as criminal suspects even when they had met all the guidelines. Policy changes in 1990 avoided the step of initial reporting to and investigation by the police; instead, the physician provides a written account of the case to the medical examiner, who then forwards it to the public prosecutor. If the criteria are satisfied, a certificate of "no objection to burial or cremation" is issued and there is no further investigation. These policy changes, however, have not altered the delicate legal status of euthanasia in the Netherlands—prohibited by law but tolerated under guidelines developed in the courts, and now recognized though not stated in the law—a delicate balance often misunderstood by outside commentators. This delicate legal status has been seen by many observers as a deterrent to abuse; it is also seen by some as accounting for a great deal of the underreporting. In any case, it is clear why the legal status of euthanasia in the Netherlands is so frequently misinterpreted by American commentators: its delicate balance between legality and illegality—the Dutch posture of "tolerance"—would be difficult to replicate in the American legal system.

2. Exaggerations Are Frequent

It is also sometimes supposed that euthanasia is a routine, frequent, everyday practice in the Netherlands, a commonplace that happens all the time. On the contrary, euthanasia is comparatively rare. There are about 2,300 cases of euthanasia per year; these represent just 1.8 percent of the total annual mortality, which in 1990 was 128,786 deaths in a population of about 15 million. In addition, there are about 400 cases of physician-assisted suicide, just 0.3 percent of the total annual mortality. Although a substantial proportion of patients, about 25,000 a year, seek their doctors' reassurance of assistance if their suffering becomes unbearable, only 9,000 explicit requests for euthanasia are made annually, and of these, fewer than one third are honored. Thus, the contention sometimes heard that there is widespread euthanasia on demand is seriously exaggerated. The actual frequency of euthanasia is about 1 in 25 deaths that occur at home, about 1 in 75 in hospital deaths, and about 1 in 800 for deaths in nursing homes.

3. The Institutional Circumstances of Euthanasia in the Netherlands Are Easily Misunderstood

Although many American observers of Dutch euthanasia risk misinterpreting many features of this practice, a particularly frequent error arises from failing to appreciate differences between health-care delivery systems and other social institutions in the Netherlands and those in the United States. In the United States virtually all physician care is provided in a professional or institutional setting: an office, clinic, care facility, or hospital. By contrast, most primary care in the Netherlands is provided in the patient's home or in the physician's home office by the *huisarts*, the general practitioner or family physician. The family physician, who typically serves a practice of about 2,300 people and is salaried on a capitation basis rather than paid on a fee-for-service basis, typically lives in the neighborhood and makes frequent house calls when a patient is ill. This provides not only closer, more personal contact between physician and patient but also an unparalleled opportunity for the physician to observe features of the patient's domestic circumstances, including any family support or pressures that might be relevant in a request for euthanasia.

Furthermore, all Dutch have a personal physician: this is a basic feature of how primary care is provided within the Netherlands' national health system. While euthanasia is sometimes performed in hospitals (about 700 of the 2,300 cases), usually when the family physician has been unable to control the patient's pain and it has been necessary to readmit the patient to the hospital, or when the patient has had extensive hospital care and feels most "at home" there, and while most hospitals now have protocols for doing so, the large majority of cases take place in the patient's home, typically after hospitalization and treatment have proved ineffective in arresting a terminal condition and the patient has come home to die. In these settings, euthanasia is most often performed by the physician who has been the long-term primary care provider for the family, and it is performed in the presence of the patient's family and others whom the patient may request, such as the visiting nurse or the pastor, but outside public view. Yet the (non)institutional circumstances of euthanasia in the Netherlands are not easy for Americans to understand: whereas dying at home is not unusual in the Netherlands (about 40 percent of Dutch deaths occur at home, and 48 percent of cancer deaths), in the United States as many as 85 percent of deaths occur in a hospital or other health-care institution, where attendance by a long-term family physician is far less frequently the case.

4. Euthanasia Isn't Routine or Anonymous

Especially in the United States, euthanasia is often understood on the "It's Over, Debbie" model, derived from the notorious account in a 1988 issue of the *Journal of the American Medical Association,* which described a sleepy resident giving a lethal dose in the middle of the night to a young woman dying of ovarian cancer—a patient he'd never seen before, whose chart he had not actually examined, with whose unidentified companion sitting by the bed he had no communication, for whom he made no attempt to provide other treatment or better pain control, and with whom he exchanged only the briefest of words.

"Let's get this over with," Debbie said, in the midst of her pain. The resident ordered a syringe of morphine sulfate drawn and—telling Debbie only that he would give her something to "let her rest" and that she should say goodbye—killed her. In fact, "It's Over, Debbie" is a virtual compendium of all that is not tolerated in Holland. Euthanasia is typically performed by the patient's personal physician, not a stranger; it is performed within the context of an extended period of consultation and care. Not only is it usually performed at home with the patient's family present, but the physician remains with the patient or in an adjoining room throughout the process. The physician takes no fee for performing euthanasia. Nor will Dutch physicians perform euthanasia for patients from other countries, with whom they have had no prior contact. Fears sometimes voiced in the United States concerning the commercialization of euthanasia or the development of a death trade, practiced for profit by greedy physicians, have no place in Holland. Euthanasia remains a rare event, generally presupposing a long-term relationship between physician and patient, and it involves an often substantial commitment of time with no financial reward.

5. There Isn't Enough Hard Data About the Practice of Euthanasia in the Netherlands

Until the appearance of two large empirical studies in 1991–1992, very little hard data had been available about the practice of euthanasia in the Netherlands, even though the practice had become open, vigorously discussed, and legally tolerated. Despite the policy that cases of euthanasia were to be reported to the Ministry of Justice by physicians who performed them, in 1986 only 84 cases were reported (now estimated to have been 3 percent of the total), and by 1990 only 454 (about 17 percent). This generated an extensive amount of conjecture about the unreported cases, variously estimated to range in frequency between 2,000 and 20,000, and invited the accusation that these cases were unreported because Dutch physicians had something to hide.

Two major empirical studies of the actual practice of euthanasia in the Netherlands were published in 1991–1992: the government-sponsored study popularly known as the Remmelink Commission report (named after Professor J. Remmelink, attorney general of the Dutch Supreme Court, who chaired the committee to which it was presented) and a dissertation presented at the Free University in Amsterdam by Gerrit van der Wal. Although the Remmelink Commission study involved a much more complex design, covered a wider range of physicians (including specialists and nursing home physicians), and received a great deal more attention than the van der Wal study of family-practice physicians only, the two studies were similar in many respects. Although their range was different, both sought to discover what Dutch physicians actually do and do not do as their patients approach death; both attempted to assess the frequency of euthanasia in the Netherlands; both attempted to assemble information about the characteristics of patients, the nature of their requests for euthanasia, and the nature of the physician's response; and both were alert to the possibility of abuse. Both studies involved surveys of physicians under the strictest guarantees of confidentiality, and both achieved high response rates. The Remmelink study included extensive direct interviews with a large sample of physicians; the van der Wal study examined police reports. Both studies were well designed, and both quite informative.

Furthermore, the two studies agreed in many of their results. Although based on extrapolations from different survey populations, they came very close in their estimates of the overall frequency of euthanasia in the Netherlands. According to the Remmelink report, of the approximately 2,300 cases of euthanasia a year, about 1,550 are performed by general practitioners, 730 by specialist physicians, and about 20 by nursing home physicians. In addition, there are another 400 cases of physician-assisted suicide. Van der Wal found a combined total of about 2,000 euthanasia and assisted-suicide cases per year in general practice alone. These studies thus revised the previously accepted best estimate of 6,000 cases a year (not to mention the extreme estimate of 20,000 cases a year) dramatically downward. Both studies agreed that euthanasia was far more frequent than assisted suicide. Both found that only a minority of requests for euthanasia are honored. Both studies examined the reasons why patients request euthanasia, and both found that pain is very seldom (about 5 percent in both studies) the sole reason, though pain is often (46 percent) one reason among others. Both found that the diagnosis in the majority of cases is cancer and that the average age of euthanasia patients is in the sixties. The Remmelink study found that euthanasia is slightly less common among men than women (48 percent males, though there was no significant difference) while assisted suicide is more common for men than women (61 percent males), and van der Wal found that euthanasia is about equal for both sexes. Both studies found that the estimated life expectancy for patients receiving euthanasia is usually a week or two, though in a small fraction of cases it is longer than six months and in another small fraction it is less than a day. And both also revealed the existence of cases that do not strictly fit the guidelines.

As extensive as the contributions of these two studies to the discussion of euthanasia in Holland have been, however, there still is not enough hard data. To be sure, some further information has become available: for example, the researchers who prepared the report to the Remmelink Commission have recently published a more intensive study of the findings in about a thousand cases that involve active termination but without explicit, current request from the patient; this took the form of three representative case scenarios. But there is not yet a broad collection of what one might call phenomenological data: interior narrations by patients themselves of their experiences as they decide to request euthanasia—perhaps available from personal journals, dictations to family members, direct interviews, diaries, and the like—that might shed further light on the nature of such choices, though there have been a few documentaries and real-life interviews (for instance, on television) between physicians and patients. A participant-observer study of euthanasia is now in progress, as well as a small, anecdotal study involving interviews of family members concerning their grieving processes following the euthanasia of a loved one. But there are neither hard nor soft comprehensive data on the perceptions of family members, nurses, clergy, or others who might have played an observer's role, nor on the perceptions of patients themselves. In short, there is still a great deal more to be learned about the practice of euthanasia in Holland. The two studies now available should be understood as crucial first contributions of empirical information rather than as the last word.

6. Terminological Differences Operate to Confuse the Issue

By and large, Dutch proponents of euthanasia use the term to refer only to what in the United States would be called voluntary active euthanasia. The term *active euthanasia* is considered essentially redundant and the term *passive euthanasia* meaningless. The Remmelink study examined not only euthanasia and assisted suicide, but also drew distinctions between withdrawal and withholding of treatment (approximately 17.5 percent of deaths) and the use of opiates while "taking into account the probability of hastening death" (another 17.5 percent of deaths). The latter phrase was chosen deliberately to cover such actions as the heavy use of morphine to control pain, even though this might depress respiration and thus bring about death, which are understood under the principle of double effect. However, the Dutch also employ the term *levensbeeindigend han-*

delen ("life-terminating acts") to refer to practices that result in the death of the patient but cannot be considered voluntary active euthanasia; this term is sometimes used broadly to encompass all withholding or withdrawing treatment, including, for instance, that in severely defective newborns, permanent coma patients, and psychogeriatric patients (all of these are situations in which withholding or withdrawing treatment is also frequent in the United States), and it is sometimes used (as in the Remmelink study) to refer to direct termination. The Remmelink researchers defined a category of practices they more narrowly called "life-terminating acts without explicit request" or LAWER; this category includes the 1,000 cases (0.8 percent of the total annual mortality) of actively caused deaths where there was no current, explicit request. Since these cases do not fit the criteria for euthanasia, they are not labeled by that term. Thus, the claim that there is no nonvoluntary active euthanasia in Holland may seem to be merely analytically true.

On the other hand, it is clear that claims by some of the more vocal opponents of euthanasia also rest on terminological confusion. For instance, Dutch cardiologist Richard Fenigsen's assertion that involuntary euthanasia outside the guidelines is widespread rests on his conflating what in the United States would be called active and passive euthanasia: Fenigsen, like many others of the opposition, does not always distinguish between causing death and withholding or withdrawing treatment, that is, what we call "allowing to die." In the United States, withholding or withdrawal of treatment, including respiratory support, antibiotics, chemotherapy, cardiopulmonary resuscitation, and artificial nutrition and hydration, tends to be regarded as morally acceptable in certain circumstances, even when these decisions are not actually made by the patient but by second parties, perhaps following the patient's antecedent wish (a view reflected in many of the cases from *Quinlan* to *Cruzan*), whereas, on the other hand, the direct causing of death, even at the current explicit request of the patient, is regarded as problematic in the extreme. In the Netherlands, the view tends to be the other way around. One suspects that much of the opposition in Holland to active voluntary euthanasia has actually been opposition to passive nonvoluntary euthanasia, a practice much more accepted in the United States than in the Netherlands. It is often said in the United States that the Dutch are stepping out onto the slippery slope in permitting active euthanasia; the Dutch, in contrast, think it is *we* who are already on the slippery slope, given our readiness to "allow to die" in ways that are not voluntary on the part of the patient. As the Dutch now begin more open discussion of decision-making concerning incompetent patients, they are entering a territory already heavily discussed in the United States in the cases from *Quinlan* to *Cruzan;* as Americans begin to debate the issues in first party choices of euthanasia or assisted suicide, we are entering territory already well familiar to the Dutch.

7. The Dutch Don't Want to Defend Everything

The Dutch are sometimes accused of being self-serving or, alternatively, of being self-deceived in their efforts to defend the practice of euthanasia. To be sure, not all Dutch accept the practice. There is a vocal group of about a thousand physicians adamantly opposed to it, and there is some opposition among the public and within specific political parties (in particular, the Christian Democratic Party, which has for years controlled the Netherlands' coalition government) and religious groups (especially the Catholic church). Yet the practice is supported by a majority of the Dutch populace (rising from 40 percent in 1966 to 78 percent in 1992) as well as a majority of Dutch physicians. Of physicians interviewed for the Remmelink study, 54 percent said they had practiced euthanasia at the explicit and persistent request of the patient or had assisted in suicide at least once (62 percent of the general practitioners, 44 percent of specialists, and 12 percent of nursing home physicians), and only 4 percent said they would neither perform euthanasia nor refer a patient to a physician who would. In the words of the Remmelink Commission's comment on the report, "a large majority of physicians in the Netherlands see euthanasia as an accepted element of medical practice under certain circumstances."

But this is not to say that the Dutch seek to whitewash the practice. They are disturbed by reports of cases that do not fit the guidelines and are not explained by other moral considerations, although these may be quite infrequent. Of the approximately 1,000 cases of active termination in which there was no explicit, current request—the LAWER cases—36 percent of patients were competent, the physician knew the patient for an extended period (on average, 2.4 years for a specialist physician, or 7.2 years for a *huisarts* or general practitioner), and in 84 percent life was shortened somewhere between a few hours and a week. Because there was no current, explicit request, these cases are sometimes described in the United States as cold-blooded murder, yet most are explained by other moral considerations. Of these 1,000 cases, according to the Remmelink researchers in both the initial and supplementary reports, about 600 did involve some form of antecedent discussion of euthanasia with the patient. These ranged from a rather vague earlier expression of a wish for euthanasia, as in comments like "If I cannot be saved anymore, you must give me something," or "Doctor, please don't let me suffer for too long," to much more extensive discussions, yet still short of an explicit request. (Thus, these cases are best understood in a way that approximates them to advance-directive cases in other situations.) In all other cases, discussion with the patient was no longer possible. In almost all of the remaining 400 cases, there was neither an antecedent nor current request from the patient, but at the time of euthanasia—"possibly with a few exceptions"—the patient was very close to death, incapable of communication, and suffering grievously. For the most part, this occurred when the patient underwent unexpectedly rapid deterioration in the final stages of a terminal illness. (These cases are best understood as cases of mercy killing, with emphasis on the motivation of mercy.) In these cases, the report to the Remmelink Commission continued, "the decision to hasten death was then nearly always taken after consultation with the family, nurses, or one or more colleagues." Most Dutch also defend these cases, though as critics point out, the danger here is that the determination of what counts as intolerable suffering in these cases is essentially up to the doctor.

Direct termination of life is also performed in a handful of pediatric cases, about ten a year, usually involving newborns with extremely severe deficits who are not in the ICU and from whom, therefore, life-prolonging treatment cannot be withdrawn. These cases are regarded as difficult and controversial. Equally controversial—and as rare or rarer—are cases concerning patients in permanent coma or persistent vegetative state; patients whose suffering, though intolerable and incurable, is mental rather than physical; and patients who have made explicit requests for euthanasia by means of advance directives, but after becoming incompetent no longer appear to be suffering.

The Remmelink study also provided some suggestion, though no clear evidence, that there may be a small fraction of cases in which there is no apparent choice by the patient and in which a merciful end of suffering for a patient *in extremis* is not the issue. These cases do disturb the Dutch: they are regarded as highly problematic, and it is clearly intended that if they occur, they should be stopped. In the Remmelink study, interviews with physicians revealed only two instances, both from the early 1980s, in which a fully competent patient was euthanized without explicit consent; in both, the patient was suffering severely. In the Remmelink study interview, the physician in one of these cases indicated that under present-day circumstances, with increased openness about these issues, he probably would have initiated more extensive consultations. There is no evidence of any patient being put to death *against* his or her expressed or implied wish.

The Dutch also distinguish between procedural and substantive or material failures to meet the guidelines, regarding the latter as much more problematic than the former. They note that failure to meet the procedural requirements of the guidelines is not uncommon; for instance, according to van der Wal, only 75 percent of family doctors asked another doctor for a second opinion, slightly fewer than half (48 percent) had kept written records, and 74 percent had issued a false death certificate stating that the death was due to natural causes. Only around a quarter had reported performing euthanasia to the Ministry of Justice, and as van der Wal pointed out, "cases that reveal shortcomings are hardly ever reported to the Public Prosecutor." Procedural failures do not particularly trouble the Dutch, but they are alert to cases in which euthanasia was performed against the wishes of the patient or for ulterior reasons. Neither study yielded concrete information about any such cases, although neither study denied that such cases ("a few exceptions") might occur.

To understand how the Dutch defend their practice of euthanasia, given the possibility of such cases, a domestic analogy may be helpful. We, like the Dutch, recognize and defend the practice of marriage: it is enshrined in our law, our religions, and our cultural norms. Among other things, we understand this practice to be quintessentially voluntary: in order to marry, the parties involved must each choose freely to do so, and their signatures on the marriage license serve to attest to this fact. But we also recognize that some marriages are not voluntary: shotgun weddings, for example, in which the groom has been threatened by the father of the pregnant bride or in which the bride sees no alternative to marrying the man who has impregnated her. Yet although we recognize that physically or socially coerced marriages do occur from time to time, we continue to defend the institution of marriage, claiming that coerced marriages aren't really central to the practice we otherwise respect. The Dutch attitude toward euthanasia is a bit like this, though coerced marriages are no doubt a good deal more frequent than problematic cases of euthanasia: it is the *practice* that is defended, not each single case that occurs within or around it. On the contrary, the Dutch seek to control these few problematic cases on the fringes—that is part of the point of bringing the practice out into the open. The Dutch government has recently indicated its intention that physicians performing LAWER will as a rule be prosecuted (though this does not guarantee that all prosecutions will result in conviction), presumably as a way of asserting more thorough control over this practice and eliminating the risk of abuse.

8. There Are No "Indications" for Euthanasia

In the Netherlands, euthanasia is understood by definition to mean voluntary euthanasia, and nonvoluntary practices, such as the thousand cases of "life-terminating acts without explicit request," are not grouped under this term. Nor are the two additional categories of practices, mentioned earlier, which were treated as distinct "medical decisions concerning the end of life" in the Remmelink and van der Wal reports (as they are also in the United States): doses of opiates intended to relieve pain but which, foreseeably, may shorten life; and discontinuations or withholdings of treatment, even when death is likely to be the outcome. But although patient choice is a necessary condition for euthanasia, it is not a sufficient condition; the patient who requests euthanasia is not thereby guaranteed it and does not oblige a physician to perform it. Indeed, according to both empirical studies, the majority of requests for euthanasia (60–67 percent) are turned down.

This situation, however, has led some observers to wonder whether there isn't a set of criteria developing for the performance of euthanasia that could in effect serve as indications. If physicians reject up to two-thirds of the requests for euthanasia, it is argued, they must be entertaining some set of criteria according to which some cases are to be accepted and others rejected—criteria other than patient choice. But if this is so, it is argued, it may invite a certain readiness to perform euthanasia whenever these criteria are met, independent of the patient's choice. The Dutch would reply by arguing that there are no positive criteria for euthanasia, but that there are indeed negative criteria for when it is *inappropriate* to perform euthanasia—for example, when the request is motivated by depression or when suffering can be relieved by other means acceptable to the patient. Without positive criteria, "indications" for euthanasia cannot develop: that is, factors in the presence of which the physician ought to perform euthanasia and hence ought to "see to it" that the patient accepts this recommendation. While some Dutch physicians say they do sometimes introduce the topic of euthanasia if the patient has not raised it, they insist that it be performed only at the patient's *request,* not as the result of consent to a procedure the physician has proposed. However, whether criteria are developing—perhaps under the guise of justifications—for life-terminating acts without explicit request, or LAWER, is another matter, perhaps the central (though not fully articulated) issue in the ongoing debate about how life may best end for incompetent patients, since in these cases patient choice is not possible anymore.

9. The Dutch See the Role of Law Rather Differently

Not only is Dutch law a civil law system rather than a common law one; not only does it contain the distinctive Dutch doctrine involving practices that are statutorily illegal but *gedogen,* or tolerated, by the public prosecutor, the courts, or both; and not only does it involve very little medical malpractice activity, but the Dutch also tend to see law as appropriately formulated at a different point in the evolution of a social practice. Americans, it is sometimes said, *begin* to address a social issue by first making laws and then challenging them in court to fine-tune and adjust them; the Dutch, on the other hand, allow a practice to evolve by "tolerating" but not legalizing it, and only when the practice is adequately controlled—when they've got it right, so to speak—is a law made to regulate the practice as it has evolved. That the Dutch do not yet have a law fully shaped to accommodate their open practice of euthanasia may not show, as some have claimed, that they are ambivalent about the practice, but perhaps rather that they are waiting for the practice to evolve to a point where it is under adequate, acceptable control, at which time it will be appropriate to finally revise the law. Both early and recent attempts to completely legalize euthanasia have failed to satisfy enough parties (especially the Christian Democrats) within the Dutch coalition governments, though the 1993 changes, if passed, will provide much more protection than previously to both physicians and their patients. Some observers still think that there will be greater agreement before long, reflecting the end of the debate and the emergence of a social consensus. Of course, some commentators see the delicate balance in which the practice is technically illegal under Dutch law but also legally protected from prosecution by Dutch court decisions and legal policy as a desirable bulwark against abuse, but others argue for a more comprehensive revision of the statute, amending the penal code and spelling out in the Medical Practice Act the conditions under which a physician could not be prosecuted. Full legalization, they argue, is crucial to providing legal security for both physicians and patients.

It has also often been suggested that it is not the delicate legal situation of euthanasia—tolerated by the courts, yet still technically prohibited by the law—that accounts for the underreporting of actual cases of euthanasia, but that the unreported cases were different and indefensible. Now, however, we know what the unreported cases are. Both the Remmelink and the van der Wal studies provide extensive detail about such cases, since they explored both reported and unreported cases. According to van der Wal, whose study included police reports among the sources of data, the reported cases and the unreported cases described by doctors in responding to the questionnaires differed with regard to procedural matters; the cases not reported tended to be those not meeting the procedural requirements, but the reported and unreported cases closely resembled each other in satisfying the substantive requirements concerning voluntariness, adequate information, the presence of intolerable suffering, and the absence of any acceptable alternatives for treatment. Thus, the unreported cases are those in which there are only procedural lapses to hide, not cases in which there is any greater frequency of substantive irregularities. The number of cases reported is currently climbing rapidly, partly due to simplified procedures and the requirement being dropped for investigation of the physician and the relatives by the police. In 1992, with simplified procedures, reporting reached almost half: 1,318, or 49 percent of the estimated total cases.

10. The Economic Circumstances of Euthanasia in the Netherlands Are Also Easily Misunderstood

The Netherlands' national system of mixed public and private health insurance provides extensive care to all patients—including all hospitalization, nursing home care, home care, and the services of physicians, nurses, physical therapists, nutritionists, counselors, and other care providers, both in institutional settings and in the home. Virtually all residents of the Netherlands, 99.4 percent, are comprehensively insured for all medical expenses (those who are not are those who, with incomes above a stipulated level, are wealthy enough to self-insure), and 100 percent are insured for the costs of long-term illness. All insurance, both public and private, has a mandated minimum level that is very ample. Americans who raise the issue of whether some patients' requests for euthanasia are motivated by financial pressures or by fear of the effect of immense medical costs to their families are committing perhaps the most frequent mistake made by American observers: to assume that the choices of patients in the Netherlands are subject to the same pressures that the choices of patients in the United

States would be. While there may be some administrative changes in the national health insurance system in the Netherlands in the near future, cost pressures on the system as a whole are met by rationing and queuing (neither currently severe), not by exclusion of individuals from coverage or by increased costs to patients. The costs to oneself or one's family of an extended illness, something that might make euthanasia attractive to a patient in the United States, are something the Dutch patient need not consider.

II. Differences in Social Circumstances Often Go Unnoticed

In American discussions of euthanasia, considerable emphasis is placed on slippery slope arguments, pointing out risks of abuse, particularly with reference to the handicapped, the poor, racial minorities, and others who might seem to be ready targets for involuntary euthanasia. The Netherlands, however, exhibits much less disparity between rich and poor, has much less racial prejudice, virtually no uninsured people, and very little homelessness. These differences underscore the difficulty both of treating the Netherlands as a model for the United States in advocating the legalization of euthanasia and also of assessing the plausibility of slippery slope arguments opposing legalization in the United States.

12. The Situation Isn't Getting Worse; It's Getting Better

Many of the foreign commentators have interpreted those cases of which the Dutch are not proud and do not wish to defend as evidence that the Dutch are indeed sliding down the slippery slope, moving from sympathetic cases of voluntary euthanasia to morally indefensible, broader-scale killing motivated by such matters as impatience, money, or power. They cite several celebrated outlier cases involving

gross violations of the guidelines, such as an infamous
nursing-home case in which nurses administered euthanasia to a group of terminally ill, mentally disturbed cancer
patients when a physician refused to do so, and the cases
the Remmelink Commission report identified as falling outside a strict interpretation of the guidelines. The recognition that there are cases of life-terminating acts without
explicit request, or LAWER, not counted as euthanasia con-
tributes to this view. Furthermore, several commentators—
especially Carlos Gomez and John Keown—have argued
that the Netherlands' legal and other protections against
future abuse are wholly inadequate.

But the Dutch themselves see things in quite a different
way: that bringing euthanasia and related practices out
into the open is a way of gaining control. For the Dutch,
this is a way of identifying a practice that, in the Netherlands as in every other country (including the United
States), has been going on undercover and entirely at the
discretion of the physician. It brings the practice into public
view, where it can be regulated by guidelines, judicial scrutiny, and the collection of objective data. It is not that the
Dutch or anyone else have only recently begun to practice
euthanasia for the dying patient, nor is this a new phenomenon in the last decade or so; rather, the Dutch are the first
to try to assert formal public control over a previously hid-
den practice and, hence, to regulate it effectively. Both open
public discussion and the development of formal mechanisms such as guidelines, hospital protocols, and reporting
requirements are seen as crucial in developing a social consensus, understood and accepted by both physicians and
patients, about what can and cannot be permitted.

These dozen caveats are intended to point to differences
between the American and Dutch health care climates that
are often unnoticed in the discussion of euthanasia, although they are only a few of the principal cautions that
should be exercised in entering this discussion. There are a
great many other differences between the United States and

the Netherlands that pose further risks of misinterpretation and misunderstanding; however, because these two highly sophisticated, industrialized, modern nations resemble each other in so many ways—including the general forms of their economic systems, their common cultural roots in the European Enlightenment, their sophisticated medical systems, and so on—these differences often go unnoticed. It is unlikely that Americans can fully understand why the Dutch support their practice of euthanasia, and conversely, it is unlikely that the Dutch will understand why the Americans are so ambivalent about its legalization or why they are so likely to distort the Dutch practice, until these differences are incorporated into both sides of the debate. In doing this, our principal problem is to detach ourselves from the antecedent biases we Americans bring to this issue, rooted in our own troubled health-care climate, and to examine Dutch practices and the reasons for them with comparatively open minds.

The Slippery Slope of Euthanasia

Nat Hentoff

A nationally syndicated columnist and social critic, Nat Hentoff has long taken a particular interest in bioethical issues. This item appeared on the op-ed page of the *Washington Post* in October 1992.

In debates with those bioethicists and physicians who believe that euthanasia is both deeply compassionate and also a logical way to cut health care costs, I am invariably scorned when I mention "the slippery slope." When the states legalize the deliberate ending of certain lives—I try to tell them—it will eventually broaden the categories of those who can be put to death with impunity.

I am told that this is nonsense in our age of highly advanced medical ethics. And American advocates of euthanasia often point to the Netherlands as a model—a place where euthanasia is quasi-legal for patients who request it. But two physicians must be convinced the patient will not recover or is in intractable pain. With such safeguards, there can be no slope, slippery or otherwise.

Yet the September 1991 official government Remmelink Report on euthanasia in the Netherlands revealed that at least 1,040 people die every year from *involuntary* euthanasia. Their physicians were so consumed with compassion that they decided not to disturb the patients by asking their opinion on the matter.

Now the slope has become more slippery in the Netherlands. The Dutch Pediatric Association's panel on neonatal ethics has asked the government to permit euthanasia for infants so damaged that their "quality of life" is low. Says Dr. Zier Versluys, chairman of the group: "It's not always good to prolong someone else's life, because life is not always good."

With that advance in medical ethics, the slope has become a chasm. Over the years in this country, I have come to know a number of people who, at birth, were condemned to death by physicians because of their very poor "quality of life" to come, but whose parents refused that compassionate advice. One of the survivors is a psychologist working with the disabled; another is a lawyer for an insurance company.

Meanwhile, anticipating some misguided criticism, Walter Nagel, secretary of the Dutch Society for Voluntary Euthanasia, says of the proposal to terminate handicapped infants: "We do not consider this as euthanasia, because euthanasia is considered here in the Netherlands as a request for the termination of life. Newborns, of course, cannot make a request. So the term euthanasia is incorrect in this case."

On Nov. 3, voters in California will have a chance to legalize euthanasia—though not yet of infants. Californians Against Human Suffering has succeeded in placing on the ballot Proposition 161: "The California Death With Dignity Act." The sponsors are careful not to use the word "euthanasia." What this merciful measure would provide is "aid in dying."

If a patient desires to end his or her life, two doctors will first have to conclude that the patient has less than six months to live. (As many doctors will attest, this sort of prediction can be alarmingly imprecise.) The two doctors, by the way, can include anyone with a medical degree who is licensed in California—a dermatologist or a plastic surgeon, for instance. The attending physician also has to determine that the patient is mentally "competent." But there is no requirement that the physician get the opinion of a psychiatrist or psychologist. (The Death With Dignity Act says only that the physician "may" request such a consultation.)

One of the grave problems with clinical depression is that many physicians cannot recognize it in a patient. Another problem is that unless it is treated, some of the depressed think obsessively about suicide. The "California Death

With Dignity Act" would facilitate more suicides of patients—with a doctor's help—before they can get out of their depressions.

There is much more reckless cheapening of life in the act, including this invitation in the official wording of the measure by the attorney general of California: "This measure would result in some unknown savings due to decreased utilization of the state Medi-Cal program and other programs, including county programs."

Savings will also result, of course, for overburdened families of the chronically ill. And the burden that the ill place on their families often creates considerable guilt in those who are sick, particularly the elderly. If California becomes the first place in the world to license its physicians to provide aid in dying and thereby relieve this guilt, the state will indeed have created a stunningly steep slope.

The American Civil Liberties Union of Southern and Northern California is supporting the euthanasia initiative. I wonder how members of that ACLU feel about also legalizing the dispatching of handicapped infants.

Euthanasia—The Need for Procedural Safeguards

Guy I. Benrubi

Guy I. Benrubi is a physician who often writes about issues in death and dying. He is a professor at the University of Florida Health Sciences Center in Jacksonville. This article originally appeared in the *New England Journal of Medicine* in 1992.

Active euthanasia is the deliberate termination of a patient's life in order to prevent further suffering. In ethical discussions this has been seen as different from the withholding of life-sustaining treatment or the administration of a drug, such as morphine, that may hasten death but that has another primary purpose.

Over the years, a large body of literature has been published for and against active euthanasia. The discussion turns on the tension between the ethical imperative to alleviate suffering, particularly in terminally ill patients who make a conscious decision to end their lives, and the proscription against participation by physicians and other health professionals in the taking of a life. Arguments for the legalization of active euthanasia center on the magnitude of suffering and autonomy of the patient. Arguments against it center on the sanctity of life as well as on the disruptive and dislocating social results if the taboo against killing were to be disregarded even in cases in which suffering would be alleviated. Further arguments use the "slippery slope" concept and focus on the concern that once active euthanasia is allowed in some cases, it will be allowed in cases that are not clear-cut and in which the concern for the person is not uppermost.

Possible models of active euthanasia are provided by the Dutch experience. In contrast, the experience in China has been cited as a model to avoid. In the Netherlands, although euthanasia is not legal, tacit agreements have developed between the medical profession and the prosecuting attorneys of the Dutch states. If certain strict guidelines are followed, physicians who participate in active euthanasia will not be prosecuted. These guidelines require that the patient be competent; that there be documentation that the patient has requested euthanasia voluntarily, consistently, and repeatedly, over a reasonable time; that the patient be suffering intolerably with no prospect of relief; and that euthanasia be performed by a physician in consultation with another physician not involved in the patient's case. In Chinese hospitals, by contrast, active euthanasia is performed on neonates (Wikler D. University of Wisconsin: personal communication). Because of concern about the expansion of the population, Chinese couples are allowed only one child, and abnormal children are often abandoned by their parents at the nursery. These children are killed there, since they have no other place to go. This model has been decried by most Western thinkers, and it is a prime example of what many fear will be the end result if we embark on the slippery slope of legalized euthanasia.

Rather than reiterate all the arguments for and against active euthanasia, I would like to present one further argument for allowing euthanasia in certain limited cases and then outline a model for possible application within the traditions of American medicine.

The ethical dilemma posed by the request for euthanasia is acute for physicians who use the latest medical techniques to care for patients who have terminal disease with a rapid course. This is particularly true for oncologists and neurologists, who deal with progressively debilitated and pain-racked patients who have no prospect of cure. In the case of certain diseases, the patient would die rapidly if medicine's full armamentarium were not used. For many such patients, we use all the latest technological measures to give them a remission or a prolonged period free from progression of their disease. We use chemotherapy, blood transfusion, immunotherapy, radiation therapy, interventional radiology, and palliative surgical procedures. With these approaches we frequently prolong life from an expected few months to many years. At some point, however, all this technology begins to fail, the patient begins to get sicker, and instead of prolonged remission, there is prolonged suffering. Were it not for our marvelous intervention, the patient would have died much more rapidly earlier on.

The situation is analogous to that of a parent who encourages a child to climb higher and higher up a tree, telling the child that he or she can climb forever upward without fear, until the highest branch is reached. Finally, the child arrives at the top of the tree, but cannot get down without the parent's help. At that point the parent says, "I am sorry, I got you up there, but I will not help you come down."

Likewise, in a patient with a metastatic sarcoma of the uterus, physicians use various chemotherapeutic and radiologic interventions to treat a lethal disease that in most cases causes death within 6 months, and the patient may still be alive 2½ years after the diagnosis. In effect, however, although we prolong life, we also prolong agony, and when the agony becomes unbearable we offer no help. The patient's disease is terminal, yet it is not killing her. It does not spread to her lungs or her liver, but to her bones, her breasts, and her soft tissues, causing discomfort, pain, and mutilation without terminating her life. She is lucid, intelligent, and suffering from pain. She wants this process to end, yet we do not help her.

Similar situations arise with other gynecologic cancers. Years ago, death from advanced cervical cancer was caused by obstructive uropathy due to ureteral blockage. Patients died a relatively merciful death from uremia or hyperkalemia. Now, with our systems of high technology, we can prevent such outcomes by maneuvers such as dialysis or percutaneous nephrostomy. The patient lives two or more years, and they may be valuable years. Yet when she is

ultimately overwhelmed by her tumor, she dies a much
more protracted and uncomfortable death than she would
have had from uremia. As physicians, we agree that we
should try to give such a patient the additional two years of
life, but we refuse to help pay the ultimate price of those
two years when it comes due. It is my contention that since
we physicians brought the patient to the state she is in we
cannot abandon her by saying that euthanasia violates the
purpose of our profession.

Another particularly painful situation occurs when a patient is terminally ill and in the throes of death. Such a
patient may spend several days either comatose or in
agony, with the family gathered around the bedside in a
tormented death watch. In such a situation, our compassion, intuition, and common sense cry out for active intervention to stop the suffering for all. Even so, we are rightly
concerned about how to set aside the role of healer and
assume the role of terminator of life without destroying the
whole structure of medicine and the expectations patients
have of their physicians. How can one maintain the physician's role and at the same time terminate a life? The taboo
against killing is so vital to our society that we abrogate it
only at great peril. When physicians kill, police officers
steal, firefighters start fires, or soldiers attack civilians, the
social matrix dissolves. It may be too facile, however, to say
that the practice of euthanasia by doctors is antithetical to
the goals of the profession and thus strikes at the foundations of society (like a government that abuses its citizens
instead of protecting them) and to leave the discussion at
that. After all, the discipline of modern medical ethics developed because advances in medical technology created
dilemmas that traditional medicine did not anticipate. The
debate about euthanasia is a result.

Obviously, if euthanasia were to be accepted in our society, stringent procedural safeguards would be needed. In
addition to those in effect in the Netherlands, we should
consider the protection afforded by the traditional medical
concepts of certification and special qualification. In our

hospitals, physicians are limited to performing procedures in which they have a demonstrated proficiency. For instance, gynecologic oncologists may perform radical hysterectomies, yet gynecologists may not. Certain cardiologists may practice interventional cardiology, whereas others may not. Thus, if we accept that suffering may legitimately be alleviated in certain cases by active euthanasia, then we can use the same process to develop a "specialty" of physicians who alone would be empowered to perform this procedure. Just as with other processes of special qualification and certification, this medical intervention would be limited to certain physicians. Two types of participants would be needed. One would be certified specialists skilled in relieving suffering and, when necessary, terminating life painlessly. The physicians most qualified would probably be anesthesiologists with special qualifications in pain management. A patient asking for active euthanasia would be referred to such a physician. If therapy failed to relieve severe pain and the patient continued to request euthanasia, then the procedure would be performed.

The second type of participant would be psychiatrists. They would provide one further safeguard, in that at least three physicians would be involved: the physician delivering medical care, the anesthesiologist, and the psychiatrist. The psychiatrist would be needed to conduct a complete evaluation of the patient, to try to determine whether the request for euthanasia was made from a relatively rational standpoint, as opposed to a state of pathologic depression. In a terminally ill patient, the distinction between pathologic depression and appropriate depression is difficult to make. Psychiatrists participating in this process should have an interest in working with such patients. Although the psychiatric evaluation would be a necessary component of the process, the psychiatrist would not have veto power over the decision to perform euthanasia. That decision would be left to the patient and the anesthesiologist.

The approach outlined here addresses a problem likely to become even more prevalent as technology advances—

namely, the pointless prolongation of agony. It would be unethical, I believe, for our profession to bring patients to a state of extended suffering and then abandon them there. Yet the threat to the integrity of the profession is real if euthanasia becomes standard practice. A safeguarding process involving certification and special qualification may address this threat. The medical profession needs to deal with the question; as many polls have shown, the public is out in front of medicine on this issue.

Part IV

NORTHWEST PASSAGE:
Debate on the Pacific Coast

This brace of articles traces the evolution of the euthanasia and assisted suicide debate on the Pacific Coast, one that took place through a series of ballot initiatives in California, Washington, and Oregon. The process culminated in November 1994 with the passage in Oregon of the first assisted suicide law in the world. Advocates had successfully charted a strategy of going over the heads of the supposed experts in medicine and ethics and directly to the people. However, opponents immediately took the measure to court on constitutional grounds.

In anticipation of the possible passage of the euthanasia initiative in Washington State, physician Robert I. Misbin raised a number of pertinent questions about its implications for the practice of medicine. These include its effect on the terminally ill and whether it would lead to involuntary euthanasia. Although the Washington measure was not limited to physician-assisted suicide but would actually have legalized voluntary euthanasia, Misbin's questions are still important in the context of Oregon.

Richard A. McCormick, a Jesuit priest and theologian,

expresses surprise at the Washington measure's defeat, given the public support of the idea of physician-assisted suicide. McCormick, who opposes any form of assisted killing, seems nevertheless pessimistic about the likelihood of stemming the popular tide indefinitely, and he lists a number of reasons why. In light of the Oregon results, he has turned out to be prescient, to his certain disappointment.

A bioethicist and professor of religious studies, Courtney S. Campbell has followed the Oregon developments closely. He details the political and cultural forces that made passage of Oregon Measure 16 possible, and the legal challenge to its implementation. Among his important observations is the ambiguity about the moral and legal position of the pharmacist who would know that he or she is filling a prescription for a lethal overdose.

Physicians' Aid in Dying

Robert I. Misbin

A physician and professor of medicine at the University of Florida at Gainesville, Robert Misbin has written a number of articles on medical ethics in the clinical setting. This one was published in the *New England Journal of Medicine* in 1991.

Proponents of Initiative 119 in the state of Washington have gathered more than the 150,000 signatures required to put the initiative on the ballot in November 1991. The measure would amend the state's natural-death act to permit "physician aid in dying," defined as "a medical service provided in person by a physician that will end the life of a conscious and mentally competent qualified person in a dignified, painless and humane manner, when requested voluntarily by the patient through a written directive executed at the time the service is desired." Although the wording of the initiative does not give details about the form that a physician's aid in dying would take, promotional material distributed by Washington Citizens for Death with Dignity indicates that it would mean the administration of intravenous medication to a sedated patient or, for a patient who could swallow, the provision of a prescription for an oral overdose of a barbiturate. The request for a physician's aid in dying must be made in writing by the terminally ill patient in the presence of two independent witnesses. Two physicians who have each examined the patient must certify in writing that the patient has a terminal illness likely to result in death within six months. The Washington initiative, unlike a previous measure in California that failed to pass, does not allow incompetent patients to receive euthanasia on the basis of previously executed advance directives.

Proponents of euthanasia and physician-assisted suicide

claim that the principle of respect for autonomy requires that patients be allowed to choose the manner of their death. The principle of beneficence further requires that a physician should make a patient's death as painless as possible. A patient has the right to refuse treatment, even if such a refusal will bring about the patient's death. Many states have laws that recognize advance directives with which a patient who has lost decision-making capacity can authorize physicians to allow the patient to die by withholding or withdrawing life-prolonging procedures. The Patient Self-Determination Act passed by Congress last year requires that as of December 1, 1991, health care facilities inform patients about their right to prepare advance directives.

Physicians themselves have a long tradition of allowing patients to die. Pneumonia is said to be the "old man's friend," because it commonly occurs in elderly patients with strokes or other debilitating illnesses and, if untreated, allows the patient to die in a few days. Once the decision is made to let a patient die, however, it can be argued that the physician must make the death as swift and painless as possible. James Rachels and other utilitarian philosophers have rejected the distinction that maintains that it is morally acceptable to allow terminally ill patients to die but unacceptable to kill them directly. If a physician terminates dialysis in a patient without kidneys or disconnects a respirator in a patient with amyotrophic lateral sclerosis, death is certain to occur. Why is it not better to kill the patient quickly with a lethal injection than to cause a slow death from uremia or suffocation? To these philosophers it is not morally relevant that in one case the cause of death would be lethal injection, whereas in the other the cause of death would be uremia or respiratory failure. Another argument in favor of physician-assisted dying is that knowing that a physician will end their lives at an appropriate time could prevent patients from committing suicide prematurely. This argument is illustrated by the well-publicized case of Janet Adkins, a woman in the early stages of Alzheimer's disease who killed herself with a suicide machine invented by Dr. Jack Kevorkian.

Whether there is a moral distinction between killing patients and allowing them to die continues to be debated by ethicists. The people of Washington, however, are likely to approve or disapprove Initiative 119 on the basis of their perceptions of its likely effect on the practice of medicine in their state. Even if one accepts that there may be circumstances in which it is justified to kill a terminally ill patient intentionally, one may still oppose Initiative 119 on the grounds that it may have harmful effects on the care of other patients, on the integrity of the medical profession, or on society as a whole. The citizens of Washington are likely to look to their physicians for information and guidance about how to vote. I propose that there are seven major questions that have to be considered.

How Would Initiative 119 Affect the Care of the Terminally Ill?

If a physician's aid in dying were to become a standard part of terminal care, there is a possibility that patients might feel compelled to request it out of fear of becoming a burden to their families. The right to die could be interpreted by a vulnerable patient as the duty to die. In a society that has not been able to constrain the ever-increasing cost of health care, euthanasia and physician-assisted suicide may be viewed by some as being "cost effective." They could therefore become a short cut in the dying process and direct effort away from providing better palliative care to dying patients and giving patients and families emotional support. On the other hand, the availability of a physician's legally sanctioned assistance in dying could potentially benefit communication between doctors and patients and thus improve terminal care. Derek Humphry of the Hemlock Society has observed that the best way to get a doctor's attention is to ask for euthanasia. Physicians who view euthanasia and assisted suicide as immoral and unethical would then be under pressure to provide their patients with such good palliative care that the patients would not consider availing themselves of the other option.

Would Initiative 119 Lead to Involuntary Euthanasia?

Although Initiative 119 permits physicians to give "aid in dying" to competent patients who request it in writing at the time it is to be rendered, there is a fear that this right would be extended to incompetent patients as well. Courts have stated that the right of patients to control their medical treatment does not end when they become incompetent. Thus, it is permissible to withdraw life support from a patient on the basis of a written advance directive or the "substituted judgment" of others who are in a position to know what the patient would want. In cases of mental retardation or severe birth defects, when what the patient would want is unknown and unknowable, courts have said that it is appropriate to apply a best-interest standard in deciding about medical treatment. By analogy, if a competent patient's suffering can be relieved by having a physician administer a lethal injection, why should this treatment be denied to an incompetent patient suffering from the same illness? Killing suffering patients for their own good is the fundamental theme expressed by Binding and Hoche in *Release to Destroy Life Unworthy of Life*, published in Germany in 1920. Although few opponents of Initiative 119, if any, believe that the measure represents the first step toward the mass murder of the handicapped, it is not unreasonable to be concerned that allowing physicians to kill patients might lead to desensitization to the value of human life. Especially in a society such as ours, in which so many people lack basic medical care, there is fear that euthanasia could be used as an economic expedient. Indeed, Thomasma and Graber have written that we are already practicing a form of "social euthanasia" in this country by denying potentially lifesaving treatment to patients who are not able to pay and do not have adequate health insurance.

Is Causing a Patient's Death Intentionally Contrary to a Physician's Role as Healer?

In 1988, the *Journal of the American Medical Association* published "It's Over, Debbie," an article in which a gynecology resident recounted being called in the middle of the night to the room of a patient with metastatic ovarian cancer and administering a lethal injection of morphine in response to her request to "get this over with." The journal received letters from lay people relating stories of the long and painful deaths their own relatives suffered and praising the resident's behavior as an act of mercy. The response from the medical profession was almost universal condemnation. Particularly biting was a letter from four prominent physician-ethicists entitled "Doctors Must Not Kill." To them not only the act of euthanasia was unacceptable, but even the discussion of it. Why?

The killing of patients by doctors has been denounced since Hippocratic times, and many believe it to be inconsistent with the doctor's role as healer. Many fear that to allow a physician to kill a patient, even at the patient's request, is to desensitize the physician to the value of human life and, as Daniel Callahan has said, "to mistakenly impute more power to human action than it actually has and to accept the conceit that nature has now fallen wholly within the realm of human control." Yet there is also danger in preserving the status quo. Physicians may become desensitized to human suffering if they feel that they are denied the legal means to alleviate that suffering by a society that does not trust them. A scrupulous and compassionate physician who grants a patient's request for sleeping pills runs the risk of prosecution if the patient ultimately uses them to commit suicide. A physician who denies this request runs the risk of reading in the newspaper that the patient traveled to a strange city in order to commit suicide with the help of another physician whom the patient had never met. A physician whose patient requests aid in dying should try to find other ways, such as hospice care or psychotherapy, to help the patient deal with suffering. But if the patient insists, the physician may be put in an untenable position. The reaction of many will be to withdraw.

How Relevant Is the Dutch Experience?

The proponents of Initiative 119 can point to the Netherlands as a nation with a tradition of individual freedom similar to our own, in which the practice of active euthanasia is supported by a large segment of the medical profession and the general public. But even if euthanasia works well in the Netherlands, there is ample reason to suspect that it would not work well in the United States. Euthanasia is still illegal in the Netherlands, but it is not prosecuted, provided that it is performed at the request of a competent patient whose suffering could not be relieved otherwise. That the act is still illegal provides a safeguard against abuse that is not included in Initiative 119. More important, however, everyone in the Netherlands has free access to health care. Thus, there is no fear that a patient might request euthanasia to save family members the expense of a long illness. Another major difference is that in the Netherlands medical care is still provided primarily by family physicians who make house calls. Such physicians know their patients and families well and are in a better position to act in accordance with their best interests than are our technologically sophisticated American specialists.

Should Religious Views About Euthanasia Be Considered?

Many people object to euthanasia on religious grounds. To them the prohibition against intentionally ending human life is so strong that any relaxation of the ban on euthanasia is unacceptable. To Orthodox Jews life is of infinite value, and therefore even one minute more of life for a dying patient is also of value. Euthanasia is strictly forbidden and is considered to be an act of murder. To Christians, the prohibition against suicide and euthanasia stems from the concept of stewardship, in which God is the giver of life and only he can take it away. As its stewards, people are required to take good care of their bodies and to use "ordinary means" to ensure their health and preservation. They are not required to use "extraordinary means" in the form of treatments that are excessively painful or burdensome, or marginally beneficial. For example, a patient with lung cancer and widespread metastases would be permitted to reject the extraordinary means represented by a mechanical respirator. But what, then, should the patient's doctor do to combat the patient's pain and anxiety in the face of impending respiratory failure? According to Roman Catholic teaching, the physician would be permitted to give the patient morphine, even though such treatment would hasten the patient's death. This is based on the principle of double effect, according to which it is permissible to take an action that has some bad effects, provided that a good effect was intended. The bad effect, however, cannot be used as a means to achieve the good. Thus, the patient with cancer could be given increasing doses of morphine to control pain and anxiety, even though this treatment may ultimately shorten the patient's life. To start with a lethal dose would not be permitted, because in that case the intention would be to cause death rather than relieve suffering. Thus, the Roman Catholic position allows physicians to use effective means to alleviate the suffering of dying patients, but it does not sanction direct killing. It can be argued that in a secular society such as the United States the teachings of a particular religion are not relevant to public policy. The Constitution grants us the right to practice any religion we choose or none at all. However, this right is not absolute, and it is limited by the potential harm a religious practice may cause to other citizens or to society as a whole. To some, the practice of euthanasia is so intrinsically evil that it cannot be tolerated in a civilized society. As stated by Richard Doerflinger, associate director of the Office for Pro-Life Activities of the National Conference of Catholic Bishops: "Sometimes one must limit particular choices to safeguard freedom itself, as when American society chose over a century ago to prevent people from selling themselves into slavery even of their own volition."

If Initiative 119 Passes, Will Washington Become a Haven for Euthanasia?

If Initiative 119 passes, Washington will be the only state in the nation in which euthanasia and assisted suicide can be practiced legally. Physicians in Washington should therefore be prepared to be deluged with requests from all over the country and abroad. The Adkins-Kevorkian affair shows that some patients may be so desperate to obtain a physician's aid in dying that they will travel long distances. Similarly, Dutch physicians report that they receive many requests for euthanasia from people all over the world. For Washington to become a center for physician-assisted dying might not necessarily be inappropriate. Patients with difficult or unusual medical problems often travel to special centers for treatment. I can imagine that a patient with cancer would be willing to travel to Washington for intensive chemotherapy followed by bone marrow transplantation, with the expectation of being able to receive a physician's aid in dying in case things turned out badly. On the other hand, the situation could easily be abused. I can imagine the horror of a euthanasia clinic in Washington at which patients arrive, undergo a superficial medical evaluation, sign a form, and are then euthanized. It will be incumbent on supporters of Initiative 119 to see to it that the measure's beneficent motives are not transformed into a windfall for self-serving doctors willing to profit from the misery of dying patients.

What Legal Safeguards Would Follow Initiative 119, and How Would They Affect the Practice of Medicine?

The right-to-die movement has come a long way in teaching the medical profession that allowing patients to die without technological intervention does not constitute failure. In most cases, decisions to let a patient die can be made by the patient, the family, and the physician without judicial review. Susan Wolf of the Hastings Center has warned that the legalization of euthanasia would lead to so many legal safeguards that the rights that patients and physicians currently enjoy could be jeopardized and the care that terminally ill patients receive might actually suffer. Wolf argues that having tried for years to keep lawyers away from the sickbed, we should resist any effort that would let them back, even in the apparent interest of patients' autonomy. Her point is well taken. There may be certain rare instances in which it is morally justified for a physician to end the life of a suffering patient, but a law designed to cover such exceptions is likely to be a bad law. Some believe that it is ethical to assist a patient's suicide by allowing the patient to hoard sleeping pills. The very fact that assisted suicide remains illegal provides a safeguard against abuse. A grand jury still has the option not to indict a physician who it thinks acted beneficently to bring about the death of a patient. One might object that it is inconsistent to say that a practice may be ethical under some circumstances but should remain illegal nonetheless. Proponents of Initiative 119 could argue that it is preferable to legalize physicians' aid in dying and have it overseen by a government agency and professional ethics committees than to rely on the potentially arbitrary decisions of prosecutors and grand juries not to charge or indict physicians under certain circumstances.

Whether or not Initiative 119 passes in the November election, it has prompted an important debate among physicians about the ethical boundaries of their profession. There are powerful arguments on both sides, but in the final analysis I think Initiative 119 should be defeated. The risk of abuse is too great to justify abandoning a rule that the medical profession has observed since Hippocratic times. Ultimately, it is for the citizens of Washington to make this decision for their state. The physicians of Washington must provide information and guidance. Although the initiative is supported by many Washington physicians, it is opposed by the state medical society. If the supporters prevail, it will be their responsibility to establish procedures to protect against abuse and to ensure that patients who request aid in dying do so without coercion and only after they have considered all the other possibilities. If the opponents prevail, it will be incumbent on them to ask themselves why Initiative 119 was able to be placed on the ballot in the first place. Too many people have seen their friends and relatives endure needless suffering at the hands of their doctors. The best response we physicians can make to the euthanasia movement is to provide better terminal care. We must reject the technological imperative that compels us to use whatever treatments are available, regardless of whether they are likely to offer our patients genuine benefit. We should seek better forms of pain control and should not wait until patients are moribund before referring them to a hospice. Above all, we must recognize that dying is a part of life and should be an occasion for families to come together to express their love. In the relentless pursuit of a cure that does not exist, we must not rob our patients of this precious time. If it takes Initiative 119 to teach us this lesson, its supporters can claim a victory whether they win or lose.

Physician-Assisted Suicide: Flight from Compassion

Richard A. McCormick

A professor of Christian ethics at the University of Notre Dame and a Jesuit priest, Richard A. McCormick has forged original positions on a number of bioethical issues. This comment on the Washington State initiative appeared in the *Christian Century* in December 1991.

Most Americans (64 percent of those questioned this year by the Boston Globe and the Harvard School of Public Health) approve of physician-assisted suicide. It was somewhat surprising, therefore, that an initiative to legalize it was defeated in Washington State on November 5. The American Medical Association opposed Initiative 119, and its senior vice-president of medical education and science, M. Roy Schwarz, stated that the profession would not soon change its position. "Maybe in five or ten years, but not soon." Five or ten decades would be too soon, in my judgment. But Schwarz's prediction may be close to the mark. The medical profession is usually, and often enough properly, conservative on these matters, but one wonders how long it will hold out against proposals like Initiative 119, especially if these represent shifts in public opinion. Not long, I fear.

Initiative 119 was no surprise apparition. It represents the convergence and culmination of at least five cultural trends. If we understand these trends we should be much better able to deal with clones of 119 in the years ahead.

The Absolutization of Autonomy

The past 20 years or so have witnessed the flowering of patient autonomy as over against an earlier medical paternalism. Paternalism refers to a system in which treatment decisions are made against the patient's preferences or without the patient's knowledge and consent. It is now all but universally admitted, at least in Western circles, that individual decision-making regarding medical treatment is a necessary part of individual dignity. What is not so widely realized is that the current heavy emphasis on autonomy represents a reaction, and reactions have a way of becoming overreactions. In the religious sphere, a reaction against legalism can lead us into the dangers of antinomianism. When we try to stop being overauthoritarian, we risk becoming anarchists.

I see two noxious offshoots of absolutizing autonomy. First, very little thought is then given to the values that ought to inform and guide the use of autonomy. Given such a vacuum, the sheer fact that a choice is the patient's tends to be viewed as the sole right-making characteristic of the choice. I call that absolutization. We have seen this approach in the way the pro-choice position on abortion is frequently presented. The fact that the choice is the woman's is regarded as the only right-making characteristic. But as Daniel Callahan notes, "There are good choices and there are bad choices." Unless we confront the features that make choices good or bad, autonomy alone tends to usurp that role. When it does, autonomy has become overstated and distorted. That overstatement translates into a total accommodation to the patient's values and wishes. If physician-assisted suicide is one of those wishes, well . . .

The second concomitant of absolutizing autonomy is an intolerance of dependence on others. People abhor being dependent. Given the canonization of independence in our consciousness, "death with dignity" means: to die in *my way* at *my time* by *my hand*. Yet the Anglican Study Group was surely correct when it wrote in 1975:

> There is a movement of giving and receiving. At the beginning and at the end of life receiving predominates over and even excludes giving. But the value of human life does

not depend only on its capacity to give. Love, *agape*, is the equal and unalterable regard for the value of other human beings independent of their particular characteristics. It extends to the helpless and hopeless, to those who have no value in their own eyes and seemingly none for society. Such neighbor-love is costly and sacrificial. It is easily destroyed. In the giver it demands unlimited caring, in the recipient absolute trust. The question must be asked whether the practice of voluntary euthanasia is consistent with the fostering of such care and trust.

Have we forgotten this? I think so. Assisted suicide is a flight from compassion, not an expression of it. It should be suspect not because it is too hard, but because it is too easy. Have we forgotten that dependent old age is a call to cling to a power (God) beyond our control? I think so. Rejection of our own dependence means ultimately rejection of our interdependence and eventually of our very mortality. Once we have achieved that, we fail to see physician-assisted suicide for what it so often is: an act of isolation and abandonment.

The Secularization of Medicine

By "secularization" I mean the divorce of the profession of medicine from a moral tradition. Negatively, this refers to the fact that medicine is increasingly independent of the values that make health care a human service. Positively, it refers to the profession's growing preoccupation with factors that are peripheral to and distract from care (insurance premiums, business atmosphere, competition, accountability structures, government controls, questions of liability and so on).

Quite practically, the secularization of the medical profession means that it is reduced to a business and physicians begin acting like businesspeople. As Dr. Edmund Pellegrino has observed, they claim the same rights as the businessperson—that is, to do business with whom they choose to. Medical knowledge is viewed as something that "belongs" to the physician and that can be dispensed on her own terms in the marketplace, and illness is seen as no different from any other need that requires a service.

When the medical profession is fully secularized, clinical judgments will also become secularized. And one important outcome of the secularization of clinical judgments is an overemphasis on autonomy. In this sense the absolutization of autonomy and the secularization of the medical profession are twin sisters.

The Inadequate Management of Pain

Many people fear not death, but dying. And one thing they fear most about dying (we shall mention another below) is pain. Unfortunately, just about everything about physicians' treatment of pain is, well, painful. In a 1989 study conducted by Dr. Jamie H. Von Roenn of Northwestern University, some unsettling facts stood out. First, only one in ten physicians said they received good training in managing pain. A sign of this is that the National Cancer Institute spends only about one-fifth of 1 percent of its billion dollar budget on pain research. Eighty-five percent of doctors surveyed stated that the majority of cancer patients are undermedicated. But Von Roenn estimated that if competently used, pain medicines could relieve the agony of 80 to 90 percent of cancer patients. Before pain can be controlled, it must be recognized. Yet in Von Roenn's findings, 60 percent of physicians admitted that the inability to assess pain remains a significant barrier to controlling pain. In brief, we have poor education, poor assessment and poor management.

Dr. Steven A. King, director of pain service in the department of psychiatry at the Maine Medical Center, put it forcefully:

> The pain associated with cancer can be managed successfully in the overwhelming majority of patients. Unfor-

tunately, few medical schools and residency programs provide teaching on pain and its management and therefore many physicians are unaware of the wide array of treatment for cancer pain.

If we had better education and better pain control, much of the perceived need for euthanasia would disappear.

The Nutrition-Hydration Debate

Several prominent cases (such as those involving Paul Brophy in Massachusetts and Clarence Herbert in California) have propelled this problem onto center stage. This was especially true in the Nancy Cruzan case. People can now be maintained in a persistent vegetative state (PVS) for years by use of nasogastric tubes or gastrostomy tubes. But must or ought we do so? Few would argue for doing so when the patient has expressly declined such treatment while competent. But what about those who have not so expressed themselves? Here controversy has swirled around cases like that of Nancy Cruzan. Many ethicists and physicians are convinced that artificial nutrition and hydration are not required for persons diagnosed as irreversibly in a PVS. They base this view on the judgment that continuing in a PVS is not a benefit to the patient and therefore is not in the patient's best interests. This is my own conviction, and I wrote as much in support of Lester and Joyce Cruzan's decision to stop Nancy's gastrostomy feedings.

Others, however—a minority, I believe—view this decision in much more sinister terms. For example, some saw continuance in a PVS as a "great benefit" to Nancy Cruzan. A group of authors writing in *Issues of Law and Medicine* in 1987 stated: "In our judgment, feeding such [permanently unconscious] patients and providing them with fluids by means of tubes is *not* useless in the strict sense because it does bring to these patients a great benefit, namely, the preservation of their lives." The most recent statement espousing this view is by Bishop John J. Myers of Peoria, Illinois, in his Pastoral Instructions to health-care administrators. He argues that artificial nutrition-hydration efforts are not useless, since they "effectively deliver nutrients" to these patients, even though they do not reverse their vegetative state. To me, that judgment defines usefulness to the patient so narrowly that personal benefit is reduced to the maintenance of physiological functioning. Patient benefit is exhaustively defined by medical effectiveness alone. Other authors (such as Gilbert Meilander of Oberlin) view the cessation of artificial nutrition-hydration from PVS patients as direct killing.

I cannot argue the case further here. My purpose is to note that the overwhelming majority of people I have polled on this matter do not want to be maintained indefinitely in a PVS because they do not regard this as a benefit to them. Indeed, they are appalled at the prospect. This is the second thing people fear about dying: the needless, heedless and aimless (as they see it) prolongation of the process. And this is where the nutrition-hydration question directly touches the issue of physician-assisted suicide. If our public policies are going to mandate nutrition-hydration treatments and prevent the discontinuance of them, people will easily view physician-assisted suicide as a preferable alternative. I am compelled to note here that certain fanatical fringes of the pro-life movement are counterproductive. By saying that Nancy Cruzan was "starved" and "killed" they will drive people to embrace physician-assisted suicide.

Closely connected with the nutrition-hydration discussion, indeed a part of it, is the distinction between killing and allowing to die. I realize that certain instances of allowing to die are irresponsible (and equivalent to killing); in some cases the distinction is hard to apply persuasively. But the distinction has served us well for many decades and it would be irresponsible to abandon it. Yet it is being fudged, not least by some courts that threaten with murder charges those who withdraw hopeless and dying patients from ventilators or other life supports. Judge Robert Muir did this at one point in the Karen Quinlan case. Those who removed Karen from the respirator, he said, would be subject to New Jersey's homicide laws. When judges confuse the removal of life supports with homicide, they make homicide look all the more acceptable. One way to soften resistance to the unacceptable is to confuse it with the acceptable.

The Financial Pressures of Health Care

No one needs to be told that there is a great pressure on everyone, especially hospitals, to cut health-care costs. We are now spending 12 percent of the GNP for health care, more than any other nation in the world. Hospitals are pressured to cut costs by Health Maintenance Organizations and by Diagnostic Related Groups. Between 1980 and 1986, 414 hospitals closed, and an Arthur Anderson study predicts conservatively that 700 more will close by 1995. Acquisition decisions, hiring practices and incentive proposals are often closely tied to market forces.

Such economic pressures constitute a coercive atmosphere to the debilitated elderly and chronically ill. "Why must I hang on like this? Am I not a drain on my family and limited resources?" As Dr. Robert Bernhoft, a surgeon and president of Washington Physicians Against Initiative 119, put it: "These people [the elderly of limited means] are already under tremendous pressure to get out of the way." The next step is not a huge leap.

Dr. Peter McGough, an opponent of Initiative 119, stated after the vote: "Saying No to assisted death is not enough. Now we have a responsibility to deal with the problems that brought out this concern." The five cultural trends described above indicate (even if they do not exhaust) the problems McGough was referring to. Failure to deal with them would invite a replay of Initiative 119 both in Washington and in other places.

When Medicine Lost Its Moral Conscience: Oregon Measure 16

Courtney S. Campbell

Courtney S. Campbell is a professor in the department of philosophy at Oregon State University. His powerful analysis of the Oregon referendum is highly critical of the process. This article was written specifically for *Arguing Euthanasia*.

The November 1994 elections had political analysts using metaphors of geologic cataclysm ("earthquake," "eruption," "tsunami") to portray the meaning of the transfer of legislative power to a political party that had been in the minority for four decades. How then can one even *begin* to describe the epochal significance of one election result from Oregon, which undid over two *millennia* of professional medical ethics? On November 10, 1994, Ballot Measure 16 (formally, the Oregon Death with Dignity Act), which permits terminally ill patients to request that physicians prescribe medication to end life, was approved by Oregon voters. The injunction of the Hippocratic Oath that physicians "will neither give a deadly drug to anybody if asked for it, nor . . . make a suggestion to this effect," was deemed irrelevant for contemporary medicine by majority vote. Oregon thus became the first jurisdiction in the world to legalize physician participation in the suicide of a patient. We have entered a new world of medicine, whose moral boundaries are as yet uncharted. This essay seeks to initiate the necessary exploration.

Lessons from Failed Precursors

The story of Measure 16 actually begins as far back as July 1989, when the *Hemlock Quarterly*, the newsletter of the

Hemlock Society, announced the movement's intentions to sponsor three citizen initiatives to legalize what was called "physician aid-in-dying." The movement targeted Oregon in 1990, Washington in 1991, and California in 1992. The time frame proved be too short for an Oregon coalition to be formed and for petitions to be gathered for an initiative, and immediate efforts within the state were postponed. However, the campaigns in both Washington and California proceeded on course. In November 1991, Initiative 119 (with some modifications from the July 1989 proposal) was voted on in Washington, and Proposition 161 was put before California voters in November 1992. Both of these initiatives were defeated by a margin of 54 percent to 46 percent.

During this period, the Hemlock Society continued to be active in Oregon, submitting a bill (SB 1141) to legalize aid in dying to the Oregon State Senate during the 1991 legislative session. Although the legislative sponsors of SB 1141 included very influential senators, the bill failed to be passed out of the Subcommittee on Bioethics and Health Insurance and was never brought to a legislative vote. The Oregon legislature instead turned its attention to revision of the state's advance-directive laws, which, in the wake of the 1989 *Cruzan* decision and the Patient Self-Determination Act of 1990, had been rendered both outdated and cumbersome. This culminated in 1993 in a progressive piece of legislation, the Health Care Decisions Act, that gave expansive rights to patients to refuse medical treatment.

The failure of these initial attempts to legalize physician assistance in dying convinced supporters of the need for a different strategy, some elements of which proved crucial to the breakthrough achieved with Measure 16.

- The proposed initiatives in Washington and California were perceived as stretching voters' comfort level by going too far too fast. The concept of physician aid in dying had encompassed refusal of medical treatment, assisted suicide, and active euthanasia by physicians. Even though polls in both states, as well as national polls, showed strong support for aid in dying in principle, the voter referendums indicated a great deal of popular reticence about a workable and enforceable public policy on these matters. Thus, a decision was made to concentrate efforts on the single issue of physician assistance in suicide.

- A direct appeal to the voters through the initiative process was deemed the preferred approach for passage of legislation because the death-with-dignity issue was deemed too hot for legislators.

- Initiatives framed by the concept of death with dignity would have to be dissociated clearly in the public mind both from the methods and moralizing of Dr. Jack Kevorkian and from the ideology of the Hemlock Society, because of unfavorable perceptions of both among a substantial majority of voters. For example, shortly after the public announcement in December 1993 of the Oregon campaign for the Death with Dignity Act, an editorial in Oregon's largest (and most liberal) newspaper, *The Oregonian,* recommended that citizens "deep-six" the petition because "initiatives backed by the Hemlock Society aren't about dignified death, they are about taking lives."

- The language of the initiatives and the public discourse of proponents needed to focus on expansion of patient choice, while avoiding wherever possible the phraseology "assisted suicide." The Portland attorney who drafted Measure 16, Eli Stutsman, observed: "We aren't legalizing suicide or legalizing mercy killing. The patient is taking control." While somewhat disingenuous (Oregon, like most other states, has no law prohibiting suicide), the proponents recognized that when death with dignity and patient control was translated by the public as "suicide," the result was a substantial loss of support, ranging from between 10 to 15 percent.

Against the backdrop of these lessons, the Oregon Death with Dignity Act was drafted during the latter months of 1993. The process was protracted, at one point almost abandoned, because of substantial disputes between members of the Oregon Right to Die coalition and the Hemlock Society. The particular issues were the actions physicians would be permitted to take (especially the question of lethal injections) and the duration of waiting periods between a patient request and physician compliance. This dispute alienated the well-known founder of the Hemlock Society, Derek Humphry, an Oregon resident and author of the best-selling book on "self-deliverance," *Final Exit.* Humphry argued for a measure that would give more options to the terminally ill, including lethal injections, as well as include assistance in dying for the "hopelessly ill"; in his view, the Death with Dignity Act was a "halfway measure." Within Oregon Right to Die, moreover, Humphry was characterized as a political liability and a fringe element among death-with-dignity advocates. Humphry's public advocacy for Measure 16 was largely confined to appeals for financial support to national right-to-die organizations. The Hemlock Society played a similar marginal role in the Oregon Right to Die coalition, while contributing more than

$250,000 to the political activism supporting Measure 16.
Notwithstanding these internal disputes, the drafting of
Measure 16 was guided by an attempt to target three prin-
ciple audiences:

- Terminally ill patients, who could be
  assured of a humane and dignified exit
  from life. A constituency noticeably
  excluded were families of the terminally
  ill, and this feature was itself reflected in
  a provision of the ballot measure that
  encouraged, but did not mandate, family
  notification of a request for medication to
  end life.

- Physicians, who needed assurance that
  their overt participation in actions
  leading to a patient's suicide would be
  immune from prosecution. Moreover,
  because it would be ultimately the
  patient's choice whether to consume the
  prescribed medication at its lethal
  dosage, physicians could understand their
  role as *indirect* participation in a
  patient's death, and thus less
  professionally compromising than active
  euthanasia. A constituency overlooked
  due to the focus on the physician's role
  was that of the pharmacists who would
  be filling out the prescriptions.

- The general public, which needed to be
  able to understand the proposal without
  requiring a legal interpreter, and which
  needed assurances that the measure had
  sufficient safeguards to preclude abuses.
  Physician Peter Goodwin, chair of
  Oregon Right to Die, acknowledged that
  safeguards were a concession to public

concerns: "I feel very strongly that this is
an issue of personal freedom for my
patients. But certainly, building in
adequate safeguards will be crucial to our
success."

In the meantime, other organizations, anticipating a
1994 vote, began a process of public education and policy
development. In October 1993, the Program for Ethics,
Science, and the Environment at Oregon State University
convened a public conference on the ethical, policy, and
professional dimensions of physician-assisted suicide.
Members of Compassion in Dying, the Hemlock Society,
the Oregon Catholic Conference, Oregon Health Decisions,
the Oregon Hospice Association, the Oregon Medical Association, and the Oregon Nurses Association, as well as influential state politicians, made presentations at the
conference. This would prove to be the first and only time
members of these major stakeholder groups would meet in
a common forum for public education; soon the lines of
advocacy would be drawn.

Oregon Health Decisions (a major shaper of the Oregon
Health Plan) and the Oregon Hospice Association collabo-
rated in a yearlong process of public education designed to
foster responsible civic discourse and voter participation on
the issue. This educational effort culminated in a statewide
set of community meetings in August 1994 that elicited a
broad set of values, hopes, and fears from Oregon citizens
regarding physician-assisted death.

Even before the citizen initiative was formally announced, the Oregon Catholic Conference began to coordi-
nate the primary opposing organization, the Coalition for
Compassionate Care. The largest religious denomination in
Oregon (11 percent of Oregonians are Roman Catholics),
the church became the financial focal point for opponents
of the measure, making an unprecedented request for
money from local parishioners, as well as receiving substantial funds from national bodies such as the Knights of

Columbus and the National Conference of Catholic Bishops. The Coalition for Compassionate Care received over $1.5 million in donations for the political campaign, a substantial portion from non-Oregon interest groups.

Medicine's Conscience and Coalition Missteps

The December 1993 formal announcement of a campaign for a voter initiative on the Oregon Death with Dignity Act thus came as little surprise to many parties. The major uncertainties were whether the initiative would include active euthanasia as well as physician-assisted suicide, and what kinds of procedural safeguards the measure would require. For reasons noted above, the initiative prohibited death by lethal injection, making a distinctive break from the Washington and California proposals. This feature received prominent public attention through Oregon Right to Die and the media in the months leading up to November 1994. The proposal also did not use the language of assisted suicide, instead opting for the nuances of "prescriptions from physicians to end life."

To place the initiative on the November 1994 ballot, Oregon Right to Die needed to obtain the signatures of 66,771 registered voters by early July 1994. This figure comprises about 3 percent of Oregon voters, and though the process of signature gathering was delayed until mid-April (following approval of the official ballot title by the Oregon Supreme Court), there was very little doubt even then that the initiative would qualify. While it was not fully appreciated at the time, the debates and missteps that occurred during the signature drive were ultimately more decisive in the passage of Measure 16 than those that occurred during the general electoral campaign.

The most significant debate occurred in late April at the annual meeting of the Oregon Medical Association. Physicians opposed to the Death with Dignity Act recommended that the OMA reaffirm its opposition to physician-assisted suicide and specifically oppose the initiative. In so doing, the OMA would align itself with the policy of the American Medical Association that the role of physician as healer is fundamentally inconsistent with physician participation in suicide. This recommendation ignited a lengthy, impassioned floor debate among the voting membership, following which the OMA leadership determined that consensus was not to be found for either side. Ultimately, the OMA opted for organizational neutrality, deciding to "neither oppose nor endorse physician-assisted suicide."

That position reflected a departure not only from the AMA but also from the state medical associations of Washington and California. However, it was strongly supported by the OMA president, Dr. Leigh Dolin of Portland, who apparently did not perceive Measure 16 as raising unusual moral questions. In Dolin's view, physician-assisted suicide represented no major shift in medical practice at all: "In the real world of medicine, it's all slippery slope. Physicians are always making decisions about quality of life." This appeal to caregiver experience in the "real" world of dying and terminal illness might seem reasonable, except that Dolin went on to claim with respect to the Death with Dignity Act: "We need to hear from our patients on this. We need to hear from the people of Oregon what to do."

The epistemological insights of patients and voters into the real world of medicine were never articulated. Thus, Dolin seemed to abdicate *any* moral authority for physicians on the question. Yet, if assisted suicide really did not pose new issues for professionals, then presumably it should be treated like any other clinical matter, which is to say that the standards of good medical practice are not determined by civic vote or patient veto. I know of no other area in professional medicine in which physicians have been so willing to abdicate their authority and responsibility for decision making. The OMA's deference to patient autonomy came at the expense of the moral conscience of medicine.

The appeal to autonomy, both patient and civic, was reinforced in late October when Dolin responded indignantly to the AMA's announced opposition to Measure 16: "We'll see how Oregonians feel about outsiders trying to tell them how to vote. . . . Since [Measure 16] is an Oregon issue, it would have been appropriate for [the AMA] to stay out of it." Dolin seemed not to accept that the question of physician assistance in suicide went beyond geographical boundaries; on the contrary, the recommendation of the OMA president now seemed to be that standards of medical practice in Oregon were to be determined by popular majority vote.

There is a further irony in the OMA's purported willingness to listen to patients and voters, because it would reverse a long-standing professional deafness on the part of organized medicine to prior patient petitions. In particular, patients had repeatedly expressed complaints that medical caregivers were doing a poor job in caring for the terminally ill, through overtreatment and inadequate pain control. As one physician-ethicist, Susan W. Tolle, commented, Measure 16 "is about medicine's accumulated inadequacies in the care of the dying. It is about replacing curative treatment with comfort care."

A further problem with the OMA's refusal to assume a position was that it was *interpreted* by the public as precisely an indication of how to vote. While Dolin and others in the OMA were waiting to get their professional cues from the voters, the reasoning of the general public was that if organized medicine was not opposed to the Death with Dignity Act, then it must be something both physicians and patients could live—and die—with. Although Dolin claimed to have insight into the real world of medicine, it is clear that the OMA simply misunderstood the meaning and implications of its professional silence in the real world of electoral politics.

Deprived of a professional ally that had proven crucial in the defeat of the Washington and California referendums, the Coalition for Compassionate Care (CCC) entered the public fray initially on its own. And the CCC quickly made a strategic mistake. The misstep consisted in not challenging the Death with Dignity act publicly during the signature-gathering phase of April to July. The purported reason for this silence was that the CCC did not want to give the initiative any unwarranted publicity. In that way, the CCC's spokespersons claimed, they hoped the act would simply die from neglect and voter apathy. This was certainly wishful thinking, as voter approval of the initiative for the November ballot was all but inevitable. A more plausible defense of the CCC approach would have been to concede this inevitability and thus save energy, money, and resources for a full-scale challenge during the fall campaign.

However the silent-treatment approach is interpreted, its implications are clear. In July, the Death with Dignity Act was approved for the general election as Ballot Measure 16 with over 96,000 supporting signatures. And potential voters supported Measure 16 by a two-to-one ratio. The support levels must be attributed in large degree to the absence of any concerted public scrutiny or argumentation. The OMA was silent; the CCC was silent; and so Measure 16 was submitted to the voters almost as a stealth initiative. The support level continued to run above 60 percent when voters tuned in to the political campaign in late October, and that margin was simply too great for opponents to overcome in a three-week time frame.

An additional factor reinforced the stealth dimension of Measure 16. Because of frustration with the state legislature during its 1993 session, Oregon interest groups turned to the initiative process with a fervor in 1993–1994 and gathered enough signatures to place eighteen different initiatives on the November ballot, the most in state history. The voting population reached a satiation point; their attention was diffused and confused rather than concentrated. Had Measure 16 been one of a handful of initiatives, it would have received much more focused attention from the electorate. As it turned out, however, it made its way to the voters absent any sustained scrutiny until very late in the election season.

The Question: To Be or Not to Be?

Measure 16 posed the following question to Oregon voters: "Shall law allow terminally ill adult Oregon patients voluntary informed choice to obtain physician's prescription for drugs to end life?" I will use the concepts embedded in this question to sketch seven different parameters of the public debate.

Legal Status

Prior to Measure 16, Oregonians already enjoyed very expansive rights with respect to end-of-life decisions. As noted previously, due to 1993 revisions in Oregon's advance-directive legislation, the law already permitted citizens to refuse any medical treatment under a broad range of conditions, including imminent death from terminal illness, permanent vegetative state, chronic degenerative illness (e.g., Alzheimer's), and extraordinary suffering. Medical nutrition and hydration could expressly be refused under any of these scenarios, and a patient was assured of receiving adequate means to control pain and suffering.

This legislation—the Oregon Health Care Decisions Act—had been in effect for less than three months when the death-with-dignity initiative was announced. It seemed to many that it was premature to offer a new option to terminally ill patients when the empowering Health Care Decisions Act had had no chance to be integrated in healthcare delivery. Indeed, professional educators, such as this author, received repeated reality jolts upon learning how few Oregonians actually knew about their new rights under the revised advance-directive law, let alone had taken steps to exercise those rights. It became clear that many Oregonians were drawing conclusions regarding Measure 16 under the illusion that the *only* options they had when faced with a potential serious illness were technological prolongation of life or suicide. Measure 16 fostered that illusion by never mentioning advance-directive alternatives and rights that terminally ill persons already possessed under the law.

However, a second aspect of the question of legal status worked to the advantage of Measure 16 supporters. Their contention, made principally through anecdotal accounts rather than empirical evidence, was that Oregon law prohibiting assisted suicide as a felony was being flouted by practitioners anyway: The legal prohibition was not, in fact, deterring physicians from covert practices of assisted suicide, nor was the law being enforced. These narratives of noncompliance with current law led some to argue that Measure 16 should be approved to provide not only more patient choices but also physician latitude and public oversight. As the legal counsel for Oregon Right to Die expressed it, Measure 16 would simply "codify existing medical practice." While this could not be directly verified, proponents, caregivers, and patients nonetheless confided that law also already allowed de facto, if not de jure, the actions proposed by Measure 16. A hospice patient-care coordinator stated, for example, that death was already being hastened through use of morphine to relieve pain: "I feel, in fact I know, that the primary intent is to end the life of the patient."

Adults with Terminal Illness

The provisions of Measure 16 that qualified patients must be at least eighteen years of age and diagnosed with a terminal condition did not, by and large, become dominant in the debate. There were a couple of exceptions to this. First, an influential state senator, Clifford Trow, questioned what social attitudes about suicide would be conveyed to teens if law sanctioned professional assistance in the suicide of the terminally ill. However, this question never assumed more than rhetorical significance. Second, Measure 16 encouraged, but did not mandate, that patients notify their families of their request for a lethal dose of medication. Thus, an important safeguard was neglected: Those persons who knew the patient best and thus could best confirm whether the request for medication was voluntary or a common response of depression regarding one's imminent mortality were not required to be consulted or notified in the decision-making process.

The inclusive and exclusive nature of the "terminal-illness" provision provoked somewhat more controversy. Measure 16 defined terminal illness more broadly than prior Oregon legislation by requiring that patient prognosis be six months or less of life expectancy, according to reasonable medical judgment. Opponents commonly invoked scenarios of medical fallibility to support a concern that erroneous judgments could involve not simply months but years prematurely shortened. Others found the criterion to be too restrictive and noted that many chronically ill patients also undergo a great deal of pain and suffering but would have no recourse for death under Measure 16. The act is quite explicit that the informed request of a patient for lethal medication is a sufficient condition, irrespective of whether the patient is experiencing pain and suffering; in no instance does the act mention compassion for pain and suffering as a justifying ground for assistance in suicide.

Some disability-rights advocates also maintained that the clause was exclusionary and perhaps even discriminatory. This argument claimed that Measure 16 gave a set of rights to capacitated and functional adults that could not be exercised by persons with disabilities (for example, a quadriplegic unable to self-administer a lethal dose).

There has been and will continue to be social pressure to expand the concept of "terminal" beyond its current meaning. Since the Death with Dignity Act is a law, rather than a constitutional amendment, it can subsequently be revised by the legislature to permit assistance in suicide to patients understood as experiencing "hopelessly ill" conditions. The prospect for expansive revisions will likely come from factions of the Oregon Right to Die coalition, including the Hemlock Society, which seek to empower persons with conditions such as Alzheimer's, ALS, or multiple sclerosis with the legal rights conferred by Measure 16.

Oregon Residency

Opponents of Measure 16 raised the prospect that approval would make Oregon a magnet for persons seeking physician assistance in death, much as Michigan had been in the early 1990s, especially were Oregon to be the only jurisdiction in the world to legalize physician-assisted suicide. This concern stemmed from ambiguity about residency qualifications proposed by the measure. By Oregon law, residency status is context dependent; that is, the criteria for residency differ depending on whether a person is seeking to vote, to obtain a driver's license, to pay in-state college tuition, and so forth. In the absence of a specific context, or when there is no legal precedent (as with assistance to terminally ill patients), Oregon common law holds that declaration of intent to reside in the state is sufficient. These ambiguities raised for some the specter that Oregon would become a medical killing ground.

This question, however theoretically valid, seems misplaced as a practical matter. Any qualified patient under the new act must satisfy several other criteria in addition to residency; satisfying these criteria (such as establishing a relationship with a physician) will take time. Thus, residency status is a necessary but not sufficient condition to make a request for medication to end life. Moreover, moving to a different residence will likely be beyond the energy, resources, and resolve of most terminally ill persons. To be sure, desperate patients have gone to foreign countries in search of *cures* for illnesses. Yet this presents a quite different scenario from a situation in which a person severs all communal ties and relations and moves to a foreign state to obtain drugs to *die*.

Voluntary and Informed Choice

The substantial majority of the procedural safeguards in the Death with Dignity Act seek to facilitate the informed consent process. A condition of *"voluntary"* choice is to be protected through

- requiring two oral and one written request by a patient for lethal medication

- waiting periods of at least fifteen days between the oral requests and forty-eight hours between the written and second oral request before a prescription could be written (both of these steps aim to ensure the authenticity and continuity of the patient's request over time.)

- encouraged (though not mandatory) notification of the patient's family regarding the request

- prohibition of coercion of a patient, under penalty of a felony charge

These are vital safeguards, but I do not believe they reach to the core of the voluntariness-coercion controversy stimulated by Measure 16. A common refrain of supporters of Measure 16 during the campaign was that such option will enable the patient to die humanely without depleting family finances and other resources. The chief petitioner for Measure 16, Barbara Coombs Lee, a registered nurse and attorney, affirmed in a public debate that among the reasons to end life is a desire to avoid "becoming a burden to family members." Lee held that this reason should be respected as an expression of an individual's right to choose.

This claim can be examined in two different ways: (1) as a noble sentiment of altruism that should be praised; (2) as a subtle but insidious form of coercion through financial indigency. The central focus of the act is to offer a right to die to benefit the patient; if, however, the right is exercised for the benefit of others, then the choice may be heteronomous rather than autonomous. What began as a right to die can, through economic influences, be transformed into a duty to die.

This is a grave issue, especially in Oregon, which now is the only state that may approve assisted suicide *and* has an explicit program of health-care rationing for the medically indigent. The coupling of assistance in suicide with rationing places many vulnerable populations at great risk; as many philosophers, such as Daniel Callahan, have argued, society combines cost controls with medical killing at its own peril. The Oregon Health Plan, which currently rations health services to the Medicaid population in the state, will provide insurance coverage for assistance in suicide as a form of comfort care. The prospect that the Death with Dignity Act might be used as a cost saver in a cost-conscious environment should not be dismissed. Economists indicated that if 20 percent of Oregon's terminally ill population exercise their rights under the act, some $700,000 in state and federal health-care funds would be saved. The moral answer to medical indigency is not assisted suicide but universal health-care coverage.

Measure 16 also stipulates important safeguards to ensure "informed" choice. Following a patient request, the attending physician must disclose information that the patient will "understand" regarding alternatives to assistance in suicide, including pain control, hospice, and comfort care; the potential risks and probable outcome of taking the medication; and the patient's right to revoke the request at any time. It is medically and morally preferable to require a more demanding disclosure standard of patient understanding of information, not simply professional disclosure of the information. However, we do not have any certain method to measure patient understanding and comprehension.

The attending physician and consulting physician must also make an independent evaluation of the patient's decision-making capability, particularly to assess whether the patient may be suffering from impaired judgment because of mental illness or depression. An affirmative determination by either physician triggers a mandatory counseling referral. This provision proved to be very controversial in public discussion of Measure 16 in two important respects. First, questions were legitimately raised

regarding whether physicians trained to treat somatic illness possess the sensitive skills needed to detect psychic
impairments. There is substantial research to indicate that
depression in the terminally ill is often missed or misdiag-
nosed by physicians. Thus, as one editorial put it: "Measure
16 would give doctors licenses to help kill, because of symptoms they have not become competent enough to relieve."

Second, assessments of capability also bring the moral
boundaries of psychiatry under the professional horizons of
the Death with Dignity Act. The act says nothing about a
psychologist's or psychiatrist's threshold for determining
capability. Moreover, many psychiatrists have objected to
providing determinations of competence for criminals sen-
tenced to die. Would this same moral reticence be present
for a psychiatrist requested to provide counseling and consultation, or might it dissipate because the terminally ill
patient, unlike the capital criminal, has requested to die?
Since Measure 16 neglects the duties of psychiatrists, it is
necessary to ask whether participation by mental health
specialists would compromise the professional ethics of psychiatry.

The Physician's Role

Three major provisions of the Death with Dignity Act are
designed to ease the moral and professional anguish of physicians.

- Physicians are limited to writing
  prescriptions for the patient, which for
  many provides psychological and moral
  distance from an act such as lethal
  injection. The physician is the direct
  agent of death under the latter scenario,
  while under the act, physicians
  understand themselves as indirect
  participants in a death chosen by the
  patient.

- No physician, health-care provider, or health-care institution is obligated to participate in a patient's request. Nor, if they refuse, are they under legal obligation to transfer the patient to a participating physician. Instead, the burden falls on the patient to seek out a new physician, who may then request a transfer of records from the original physician.

- A participating physician who acts "in good faith" to comply with Measure 16 is immune from civil, criminal, or professional liability.

Despite the provision for nonparticipation, it is unlikely that patients will encounter a shortage of physicians willing to prescribe the lethal drugs. A comprehensive study of attitudes among physicians in Washington State toward "prescription of medication or the counseling of an ill patient so he or she may use an overdose to end his or her own life" indicated an approval level of 53 percent for legalization of such acts and a willingness-to-participate level of 40 percent. A survey of Oregon physicians in the state's second-largest population center (Eugene) indicated an approval level of 62 percent, although a question about participation was not asked. Thus, despite the strong denunciation of Measure 16 by the American Medical Association, there are clearly sizable proportions of physicians who do not agree that participation involves the physician in an unethical act.

For some persons, the question of physician involvement was not so worrisome as that of *which* physicians. It was often claimed that hospice physicians, with their experience in palliative care and pain control, and supported by a team concept of holistic caregiving, would make the ideal physician participants. Yet this would compromise hospice philosophy, which maintains that the goal of hospice care is neither to prolong nor hasten death. A stance of opposition to physician-assisted suicide in general and Measure 16 in particular was announced by the Oregon Hospice Association in August 1994. However, this position seemed to have little discernable influence even among the hospice community, let alone the general public. Some individual hospice programs adopted stances of neutrality on Measure 16, while others planned to offer assistance in suicide as part of hospice care were the Measure approved.

Prescriptions: The Pharmacist's Role

One of the substantial oversights of the Death with Dignity Act is that the role of pharmacists in fulfilling prescriptions is completely neglected. According to Oregon statute, pharmacy practice includes "participation in drug selection and drug utilization reviews" and "responsibility for advising . . . of therapeutic values, content, hazards, and use of drugs and devices." The physician-patient relationship that involves prescription drugs cannot then legitimately bypass the pharmacist. Yet this situation presents serious professional binds for the pharmacist. It is, first, professionally demeaning, for it views the pharmacist simply as the technical arm of the physician's practice. Yet, if presented with a prescription for a lethal dose of medication, how will the pharmacist be able to determine whether the physician and patient have complied with all the provisions of Measure 16 prior to the visit to the pharmacist? Moreover, pharmacists risk charges of unprofessional conduct in "dispensing a drug, medication, or device where the pharmacist knows or should know due to the apparent circumstances that the prescription is issued for other than legitimate medical purpose." The exclusion of pharmacists from consideration in the act is difficult to justify, given the presumption of professional collaboration embedded in the statutes. There is no requirement that physicians even inform pharmacists that a prescription is being written to take life.

This presumes the willingness of pharmacists to participate and consult, which is not a foregone conclusion. In early October, the Oregon State Pharmacists Association voted unanimously to oppose Measure 16. "Pharmacists are educated in the healing arts to prolong life in the treatment and healing of illnesses and injuries. [The OSPA] views Measure 16 as a direct contradiction to that [mission]." While pharmacists are also under no obligation to participate, the OSPA presented scenarios in which a pharmacist may be confronted with a choice between employment and professional ethics. Nonetheless, following approval of Measure 16, the OSPA developed an interdisciplinary task force to present guidance to pharmacists on compliance with the law.

Ending Life

One of the more remarkable things in the public debate about Measure 16 was the widespread assumption that the patient would self-administer the life-ending medication. There is absolutely no reference to self-administration in the Death with Dignity Act. Indeed, as indicated above, almost the entire focus of the act is directed at the physician's act of writing a prescription. The details of what happens after that—who fills the prescription and who administers it—are not addressed.

While a convergence of populist and professional forces was instrumental in the public discussion of legalization, it is nonetheless not clear just how many persons will actually use this recourse to end their lives. Extrapolating from the Remmelink study of euthanasia and assisted suicide in the Netherlands, Derek Humphry suggested that 0.3 percent of the terminally ill population in Oregon, that is, under one hundred persons, would exercise their right to prescription medication to end life. Others estimate the figure to be closer to 3 percent, or nearly one thousand persons.

Whatever the number, Oregonians will receive only a statistical report of cases from the state Health Division. The Health Division will not be required to monitor every case of assisted suicide under Measure 16, but only to review sample cases. How any review will be accomplished is questionable, since there is no provision requiring that physicians report their participation to the Health Division; the Health Division is contemplating creating a new category for deaths attributed to prescribed medication to end life so that death certificates do not have to be falsified to comply with state law. The monitoring and reporting mechanisms of the Death with Dignity Act are very lax and open to potential abuse. That would be most ironic, because supporters often argued that, since physician-assisted suicide was covertly practiced in medicine anyway, it would be best conducted in the open and under public oversight. Yet these oversight provisions turn out to be minimal at best.

Moral Authoritarianism and Autonomy

Measure 16 was approved by a slim margin of 51 percent to 49 percent, or some 77,000 votes of 1.2 million cast. The measure was defeated in twenty of thirty-six counties but carried the two largest metropolitan areas, Portland and Eugene, by 55 percent to 45 percent, and this majority ultimately proved to be the margin of victory. In our attempt to understand the approval of Measure 16, some general themes are very compelling.

First, proponents of the measure successfully exploited the hostility toward religion among the Oregon electorate. Oregon is the most unchurched state among the forty-eight contiguous states. Oregon is also home to one of the most politically active religious organizations in the nation, the Oregon Citizens Alliance, whose conservative and polemical views on many social issues have cast a moral shadow on all religious denominations and led to a deep polarization in the state regarding religion.

The Right to Die coalition skillfully used the religion issue to its advantage. It succeeded first in portraying the debate over Measure 16 as a clash between outdated religious values and contemporary secular values. A prominent campaign ad warned Oregonians, "You know, there are some people who think they have the divine right to control other people's lives." The proponents also portrayed the opposition of the Roman Catholic church to Measure 16 as a manifestation of the social agenda of the polarizing and "radical religious right" and hence an infringement on the constitutional bounds of religious discourse. Thus, when the Oregon Catholic Conference announced its opposition, the executive director of Oregon Right to Die responded: "This politicking from the pulpit clearly shows our opponents' intention to promote Catholic religious doctrine by influencing Oregon voters." What is equally noteworthy as the antireligion backlash is what the Catholic tradition did *not* do. In 1991, the Catholic bishops in Washington State and Oregon responded to Washington Initiative 119 with an articulate and widely publicized pastoral letter, "Living and Dying Well." No such document of ecclesiastical teaching emerged in response to Measure 16.

The perception of overreaching religious influence is also displayed by examining the broader context of the Oregon 1994 election. Every measure that received some sponsorship from some religious organization, including initiatives on gay rights, obscenity statutes, and pornography laws, was defeated. These issues, along with Measure 16, raised a specter of intrusion on private choices, a prospect antithetical to the independent ethos of Oregonians. Thus, approval of Measure 16 also reflected a deep-rooted rejection of moral authoritarianism, whether conveyed through religious traditions or the paternalism of the state.

Measure 16 was no less a referendum on contemporary medical practice. While the OMA opted for professional passivity and the AMA for opposition based on the physicians' role as healer, the verdict of the people was quite different from either of these approaches. Physicians were summoned to assume responsibility for care of the terminally ill, which was seen to encompass pain control, comfort care, and hospice care, as well as involvement in assisted suicide. This means as well that physician's roles as fighter against and curer of disease, which commonly ensue in overtreatment and defensive medicine, must be balanced by values of caring when cure is not possible, compassion in the face of pain and suffering, and nonabandonment of the dying person.

It would, however, be misleading to see in Measure 16 simply a rejection of religious, policy, or professional expertise and control. Measure 16 was an affirmation, most significantly, of the ideology of patient control and self-determination. This was conveyed not through erudite philosophical argumentation, however, but through poignant narratives of dying related by patients and their families. That is, the persuasive appeal of Measure 16 resided in the response of empathy to the stories of identified persons. It is striking that media coverage of Measure 16 seldom focused on questions of broad professional, ethical, or policy import, but rather on its implications for persons with terminal illness. The public debate was framed by the stories of those who, like Jann Mitchell writing in the *Oregonian*, have "heard the whisper of death's wings [and] can share their experiences and opinions." On Measure 16, patients were *the* moral authorities.

Measure 16 was personalized and given a human face by the sad stories of suffering of patients and their families. This portrayal, to be sure, elicited some outrage and bitterness against professional and religious authoritarianism, but the response elicited was primarily that of empathy and identification with the sufferer and projection of one's own life story into the scenario of the sufferer. The personalization of Measure 16 should remind us that the moral choices of the human self are both rational and emotional in nature.

Looking to the Future

Were an act like Measure 16 to become law, in any state, five issues should be given careful scrutiny in the process of implementation.

Self-Administration

The Death with Dignity Act is focused on the right of the terminally ill patient to request a prescription to end life. What happens subsequent to that act of the physician is not addressed. In particular, there is substantial ambiguity as to who may administer the life-ending medication. Although proponents claim that the law requires self-administration, no such statement is present in the act. To avoid abuse, implementing action must clarify that only the patient who makes the request has a right to administer the medication to end life.

Health-Care Providers

The roles of other participating health-care providers, apart from physicians, need to be clarified explicitly. The act lacks specificity as to the roles and responsibilities of at least two other participating professions, psychiatrists and pharmacists, not to mention nursing staff and allied health professionals. Thus, it does nothing to foster a "team" approach to care of the terminally ill. The goal of the law should be to promote collaboration, not isolation, of professional caregivers.

Oversight

Monitoring and public oversight of the act needs to be much more rigorous. It is not enough for the Oregon Health Division to annually review a sample of cases and present a statistical report to the public (assuming the Health Division can get access to this information). One lesson that should have been learned by now from the euthanasia experiment in the Netherlands is that lax reporting and monitoring opens the doors to abuse. Every case should be documented by physicians and reviewed by public health authorities, who should give a complete substantive report to the public.

Residency

Legislation needs to be developed to clarify the meaning of residency status for the context of physician-assisted suicide. While I strongly dispute the contention of opponents that Oregon will now become a "magnet for the depressed, the sick, and the bizarre of the civilized universe," the act, as it currently reads, does not preclude terminally ill persons from coming to Oregon to end their lives.

Medicine's Conscience

The medical profession and related associations must read approval of the initiative as an assessment of the current practice of medicine. In particular, medicine is too reliant on technology, very depersonalizing, and inattentive to patient pain and suffering. Those are all remediable problems if the moral conscience of medicine will appropriate the value of caring into its professional horizons.

The Legal Challenge

Shortly after the passage of Measure 16, a state-appointed task force was established to set up a new legal category for deaths that conformed to the provisions of the measure. The new category was necessary because "physician-assisted suicide" cannot legally be listed as the cause of death in Oregon; thus the required reporting of such cases to the Oregon Health Division is an impossible task. Not surprising, however, the deliberations of the task force ended without any resolution. In the meantime, debate over the Death with Dignity Act shifted from the political to the legal forum.

In late November, the legality of Measure 16 was challenged by James Bopp, Jr., of the National Right to Life Committee (NLRC), on behalf of two nursing homes. Bopp's motion requested a permanent injunction on Measure 16 on the grounds that it violated constitutional guarantee to equal protection and due process, as well as the Americans with Disabilities Act (ADA) and the Religious Freedom Restoration Act. On December 7, 1994—the day before Measure 16 would become legally effective—Bopp's motion was ruled upon and a temporary restraining order was issued by U.S. District Court Judge Michael Hogan. Hogan scheduled a hearing for December 19 to review the constitutional arguments.

In Judge Hogan, the opponents of Measure 16 had deliberately selected a sympathetic ear for their cause. While a Democrat by political persuasion, Hogan also affirms deep Christian convictions, and it was this religious background that persuaded Bopp and the plaintiffs to file their legal challenge in Hogan's court in Eugene, rather than before any of several district court judges in Portland.

In the meantime, advocates of Measure 16 were not silent. The Oregon attorney general deemed the measure constitutionally defensible and prepared to argue against the injunction. This put the state in the rather unenviable position of having to abandon governmental neutrality on the issue and to go on record as supporting the rights of terminally ill patients to end their lives with prescribed medication. Moreover, four patients (three with cancer, one with AIDS), a physician, and the chief petitioners of Measure 16 from the Oregon Right to Die coalition requested of the court permission to intervene in the hearing. Their motion asked Judge Hogan to dismiss Bopp's lawsuit because of lack of legal standing of the NLRC, and because implementation would not coerce physicians, caregivers, or patients and thus not run afoul of constitutional guarantees. To defray legal costs, supporters also founded the Oregon

Death with Dignity Legal Defense and Education Center. Following the arguments presented during the December 19 hearing, Hogan issued a ten-day extension of the restraining order. Then, on December 27, Hogan granted a preliminary injunction, which blocked Measure 16 from taking effect until he issues a ruling on the law's constitutionality under the First (freedom of religion) and Fourteenth (equal protection and due process) Amendments, as well as whether the law complies with the provisions of the ADA. Hogan stated: "Death constitutes an irreparable injury, and I find that the possibility of unnecessary death by assisted suicide has been sufficiently raised to satisfy the irreparable harm requirement for a preliminary injunction." Hogan also cited an overriding public interest in "protecting vulnerable citizens from the irreparable harm of death."

There are two very striking issues in the ruling. The first is the affirmation of death as an irreparable "injury" and "harm," which is presented as an uncontroversial position, when in fact, supporters of the measure clearly see death as a benefit and as a last means to express their personal dignity. Equally intriguing is Judge Hogan's focus on *unnecessary death* as grounds for the injunction, whereas proponents have repeatedly appealed to *unnecessary suffering* as grounds for the legitimacy of the measure. What remains uncertain is whether Hogan would find all deaths by assisted suicide to be "unnecessary" deaths, in which case Measure 16 would be found unconstitutional, or whether he is concerned primarily with unnecessary deaths for "vulnerable citizens." This approach would permit the legitimacy of assisted suicide in principle and allow its practice in those cases where procedural safeguards have been adhered to. (Some opponents, of course, have argued that no procedure can be so fail-safe as not to risk the lives of vulnerable patients.)

The response to Hogan's ruling within the Oregon medical community and the right-to-die advocacy groups has been that medical practice will revert, for the time being, to the status quo. That is, some patient deaths will occur behind closed doors, in secret, and outside the boundaries of the law. Thus, after an intense political process of several years, we still remain in the dark professionally, ethically, and legally on the status of physician-assisted suicide.

Part V

Voices For and Against

In this part of the book we attempt to take stock of some broad questions. For example, Daniel Callahan opposes euthanasia and assisted suicide but favors societal limits on aggressive end-of-life treatment. How can these positions be reconciled? He argues not only that these positions are consistent but that together they express both reverence for the sanctity of life and respect for the inevitability of death.

Dan Brock begins by reminding us of some critical distinctions, then asks what the good and bad consequences of legalized voluntary active euthanasia would be and how such a policy accords with the aims of medicine. He argues that euthanasia need not create distrust of the medical profession, and indeed that the legal right to assist in death should probably be restricted to doctors.

Reaching into our deepest cultural and theological traditions, Leon R. Kass arrives at conclusions that could hardly be more different from those of Brock. He finds no dignity in euthanasia, and a great deal of danger in opposing the idea of personal dignity to that of the sanctity of life. Yet he does not wish to dismiss the realities of human suffering, but rather to urge that they be placed in the context in which so many have lived and died.

After Kass's profound observations follow two first-person accounts of suffering whose authors favor euthanasia or assisted suicide. Philosopher Sidney Hook introduces a different cultural reference point from those to which Kass refers: the ancient Stoic philosophers. In reflecting on the value he found in his own life, he does not find suffering in old age to be uplifting. Rather, for him wisdom consists in knowing when it is the right time to die. Journalist Betty Rollin recalls her decision to help her mother, who was stricken with ovarian cancer, to obtain a prescription so that she could overdose. She also describes the public reaction to her book *Last Wish*.

Ronald Dworkin concludes by placing both the euthanasia and abortion debates within the sanctity-of-life theme that has surfaced repeatedly in these essays. He points out that the contentiousness of the public debate about these issues tends to obscure an important fact: People who favor or oppose euthanasia or abortion deeply believe that life is of inherent and unique value. What they disagree about is what *counts* as expressing respect for life.

Vital Distinctions, Mortal Questions: Debating Euthanasia and Health Care Costs

Daniel Callahan

Daniel Callahan is a distinguished bioethicist and philosopher who is president and cofounder of the Hastings Center. Much of his recent work has dealt with the
relationship between medical ethics and health-care
costs. This paper was first published in *Commonweal*
in July 1988.

The euthanasia issue is entering a new phase, one likely
to be complicated and painful. Though California voters recently defeated an initiative to put a euthanasia referendum on the ballot, public opinion surveys, here and
abroad, indicate growing support for active euthanasia and
assisted suicide. The de facto legalization of euthanasia in
Holland does not necessarily signal the beginning of a larger
trend, but its occurrence is a significant break with a long-
standing prohibition in Western societies.

This already difficult set of issues is almost certain to be
further complicated by the growing need to ration health-
care resources. The decision of the Oregon legislature in
1987 to deny organ transplants under its Medicaid program, and to spend the money instead on prenatal care, will
not remain an isolated event. Less dramatically but more
pervasively, the failure to control medical costs has stimulated a national effort to reduce unnecessary and wasteful
treatments. Medical care of the dying or the critically ill—
long believed to be a frequent source of doubtful expendi-
tures—has emerged as a place to curtail heavy medical
costs.

The conflation of the allocation and euthanasia issues is
becoming increasingly evident. On one side are those who

argue, with apocalyptic dread, that economic excuses and rigid cost-benefit analysis will now be deployed to carry out what is otherwise unthinkable: to rid our society of the retarded, the handicapped, and the burdensome elderly. David Andrusko, an editor of the *National Right to Life News*, has called this trend a "juggernaut of death." On the other side are those who argue that it is precisely the denial of a right to die that grievously exacerbates our financial plight. Patients need more power, they say, including the right to active euthanasia and assisted suicide and the means to curb the physicians' appetite for aggressive medicine regardless of a patient's prospects. As William S. Kilbourne Jr. put it in the *Euthanasia Review*, "not all the torture dealt out by all of the totalitarian governments in the world causes as much pain as overtreatment of the terminally ill."

These new developments raise two questions. Does the long-standing Western tradition that rejects active euthanasia and assisted suicide have the intellectual resources to withstand the growing pressures to legitimate them? Does that same tradition also have the resources to cope with the allocation issue, and to do so in a way that respects human life and dignity? I think that it is rich enough to encompass both problems simultaneously, but that at some crucial points it needs further work and elaboration. The tradition must strengthen the arguments against active euthanasia and, at the same time, develop morally justifiable criteria for limiting life-sustaining health care at the societal level by defining the circumstances when such limitation is necessary or sensible.

Does the Long-Standing Western Tradition That Rejects Active Euthanasia and Assisted Suicide Have the Intellectual Resources to Withstand the Growing Pressures to Legitimate Them?

What is behind the change in public opinion on euthanasia? A great deal of the emerging debate is coming to turn on not simply what is, or may be, happening, but also on what it means and how it should be interpreted. Let me venture an interpretation.

Changing Attitudes

Since the 1970s, death has been an institutional event, with over 80 percent of deaths occurring in hospitals. Even those dying in nursing homes are likely, in an acute crisis, to be taken to a hospital. Hospitals themselves have become different institutions, more than ever oriented to intensive care. Once in hospitals, patients are faced with a strong bias toward aggressive technological care. They will be treated by doctors nervous about malpractice suits, but in any case trained to save life unless there is a powerful presumption against it and, most important, increasingly ingenious in the extension of life against great odds. When a patient dies in a hospital it is almost always now the result of some conscious decision, the result of a medical power able to give almost every patient at least a few more hours or days. Patients are as a rule more quickly put on respirators than was the case twenty years ago, and they are much more likely to be fed artificially should their critical illness render them incapable of or uninterested in eating.

Beyond the hospital setting there have been other important general trends. The broadest and most encompassing is the increase in chronic illness, particularly that ensuing upon acute episodes of life-saving interventions. More of those episodes are followed by a long decline toward death, often marked by sporadic acute recurrences where the patient is brought through once again. An increase in the time between the determination of a terminal illness, or fatal disease, and death is still another important change, now reaching three years in the case of cancer deaths. An extended life with a chronic illness, and an extended dying, are growing consequences of improved medical care. As Arthur Barsky, M.D., has noted in his new book, *Worried Sick: Our Troubled Quest for Wellness* (Little, Brown,

1988), "while more effective medical care enables us to live longer, the *proportion* of life spent in ill health has actually *increased.*" It is these "failures of success" that account for the rising incidence of some late-onset diseases, such as Alzheimer's.

General public awareness of these shifts is an important reason, I am convinced, for the rise of interest in active euthanasia. Public opinion surveys have indicated a sharp shift in that direction. Comparative Louis Harris surveys show that 53 percent of respondents in 1973 opposed active euthanasia (with 37 percent favorable), while by 1985, 61 percent were favorable, with only 36 percent opposed. These changes closely parallel changes in medical practice, especially the shift to deaths in institutional settings. It is plausible to think that the public has become more fearful of an extended or painful death, and wants active euthanasia to regain mastery over medical attitudes and technologies it believes can no longer be controlled.

There is an alternative interpretation. In this view, our culture is now disposed to take the value of life less seriously than it once did. The greatest danger is not that patients will be overtreated or their lives too long extended, but that socially burdensome patients will be targeted for elimination, sacrificial victims on the altar of cost-benefit analysis. I have no doubt that the seeds of such a possibility are present—one can find some indication of just about any trend one likes in this area—but there is as yet no good *evidence* that it is strong or widespread. A reported increase in mortality rates in some places as a result of the diagnostic related groups (DRG) cost-containment strategy under Medicare is, however, the kind of evidence that should be followed.

In any event the fear of a shift to active euthanasia, a fear made more credible by the polls, has been the stimulus behind prolife resistance to almost all proposed legal changes. Living will legislation, for instance, is looked upon as the leading wedge of a value system whose acceptance will lead first to legitimating active euthanasia, and then to killing the weak and powerless. While there is now said to be less total resistance to policy change among prolife groups, and some actual recent initiatives, their political power has intimidated politicians. Within medicine, a fear of indictment in some places for termination of treatment and a more generalized anxiety about malpractice suits (however overblown in actuality) has created a climate of uneasiness. For most physicians, the course of least resistance is simply to treat, and the more aggressive their treatment, the safer they feel. Here is where things come full circle: an awareness of that physician-nervousness serves all the more to increase patient anxiety. It begins to seem that only acceptance of a policy of active euthanasia will prevent the possibility of overtreatment.

The Euthanasia Debate

While the euthanasia movement has deep historical roots, going back to Greek and Roman times, it has had a special force in the West for a number of decades (and in England since the nineteenth century). Its primary argument has always been a relatively simple one: a dying person (or one whose life has become intolerably burdensome) has the right to have his or her life ended by another if that is necessary to avoid suffering. The popular phrase "mercy killing" refers to the killing of one person by another as an act of kindness, not as an act of malice or self-interest on the part of the one who does the killing (or assists in a suicide). The moral foundation of this claimed right is that our body is our own, and that our life should be subject to our self-determination. We have, then, a right to end our own life; and if we cannot accomplish that on our own, another person has the right to end it for us, as an act of compassion. These arguments gain weight from the reality that contemporary medicine can and does draw out our dying, or our suffering lives, beyond all decent limits. That we could, by providing more choice to patients, also reduce unnecessary and unwanted costs is still another important consideration; individual and social good could be jointly served.

Beyond that plausible possibility is the further danger of a move to involuntary euthanasia. If there are some lives "not worth living"—and not just the lives of the terminally ill but of others whose quality of life is low—why not, then, for their sake as well as that of society, simply end those lives? The right to die could become a duty to die. The likelihood that society will ride this slippery slope, from voluntary to involuntary, *may* increase once the principle of direct killing has been introduced. Reasons of both expediency and mercy will have been used to make that introduction acceptable.

To all of these long-standing objections, I would add another. Precisely because of the growing need for health-care rationing, there is all the more reason to avoid the possible abuses of active euthanasia. The attraction of using it as a way of assisting cost-containment efforts would increase the risks of abuse all the more. The cleaner the separation between rationing and euthanasia, the better.

Nonetheless, more work is needed to develop the reasons for opposition to active euthanasia, reasons that do not depend too heavily on possible abuses. Those of us who use such arguments against euthanasia should realize that, for all of their intuitive plausibility, they rest upon a calculus of probabilities that has little grounding in history or experience. The often-invoked Nazi analogy has limited value for our situation. The Nazis did not start with voluntary euthanasia and move on to involuntary euthanasia; they started with the latter, and their rationale for involuntary euthanasia had nothing to do with either self-determination or the avoidance of medical overtreatment. These slippery slope arguments are, then, not fully adequate.

A traditional religious position has supplied the missing argument: self-determination does not extend to a right to take our own life; God alone has the right to take innocent life. For many, that belief remains the ground for resistance. But it will have limited force in the secular domain. We need a more philosophical argument, not dependent on religious premises, that might have a comparable force, and that would apply even if one granted that patients have a right to take their own lives (now legal in most states). If such a right is conceded, does it follow that another may be given the right to kill such patients? I do not think so.

John Stuart Mill, in his classic work, *On Liberty*, argued that the one exception to our right to do with our person as we will is the right to sell ourselves into slavery. "By selling himself for a slave," he wrote, "[a person] abdicates his liberty; he forgoes any future use of it beyond the single act. . . The principle of freedom cannot require that he should be free not to be free. It is not freedom to be allowed to alienate his freedom."

There is a parallel here: to cede to another the right to kill us is to give that person the power to remove our freedom once and for all. The reason even voluntary slavery is wrong is not simply that we ought not, in the name of mercy or freedom, be able to alienate our freedom so fundamentally, but also that no other person should be given so total and decisive a power over our life. That is the most basic threat to, or violation of, the right of self-determination that can be imagined. However strong the motive to do so, that fundamental right cannot be set aside without contradicting its very nature. If I am by right master of my fate, I cannot transfer my right of mastery to another, nor can any other person receive it from me.

To ask another to be the agent of my death, moreover, would cease to be simply an expression of my isolated autonomy. It would create a profound relationship between that other person and myself, transcending our individual acts. From the side of the person who killed me his would be an irrevocable act, one that becomes his act as much as mine. From my side, I would be recruiting an accomplice, asking him to take into his hands a decisive power over me, one that could not be recalled once he had acted. I see no moral basis for so ultimate a transfer of the power of life and death. It is more than the principle of self-determination historically has, or morally should, encompass.

Does Western Tradition Have the Resources to Cope with the Allocation of Health-Care Resources in a Way That Respects Human Life and Dignity?

The euthanasia and allocation debates are easily likely to mutually confuse, even pollute each other. To avoid that, it is necessary to be clear about the difference between directly killing a known patient and making an allocation decision whose effect will be to allow many to die who might otherwise be saved. How can it be morally plausible to condemn the one but allow the other? In the first section, I have tried to sketch, all too briefly, why I think that the traditional prohibition of direct killing has been correct: active euthanasia runs the risk of corruption and wrongly extends to another the right to control our bodies.

But of late, the strongest challenge to the tradition has been a denial that there is a meaningful distinction to be made between killing and allowing to die, between an act of commission and one of omission. While this challenge comes most strongly from those favoring the legalization of active euthanasia, it seems to draw at least implicit or inadvertent support from some prolife groups as well. Supporters of euthanasia argue that if there is no serious distinction to be drawn between killing and allowing to die, then our present acceptance of allowing to die ought to be extended to active killing, when such killings would be more merciful. Prolife groups may acknowledge a strictly logical distinction between the two, but argue that "allowing to die" is a slogan that has come to be used as a legitimizing rationale to end the lives of those who are burdensome or judged to have lives not worth living. This simultaneous challenge from the liberals and the conservatives promises maximum confusion, making it that much harder to discuss carefully the euthanasia issue and all but impossible to consider coherently the allocation problem.

Maintaining the Distinction

My contention is that, properly understood, the distinction between killing and allowing to die is still perfectly valid for use, both in the euthanasia debate and in the allocation discussion. The distinction rests on the commonplace observation that lives can come to an end as the result of *(a)* the direct action of another who becomes the cause of death (as in shooting a person), or as the result of *(b)* impersonal forces where no human agent has acted (death by lightning or by disease).

The purpose of the distinction is to separate those deaths directly caused by human action, and those caused by nonhuman events. It is, as a distinction, meant to say something about human beings and their relationship to the world. It attempts to articulate the difference between those actions for which human beings can rightly be held responsible and those of which they are innocent. At the heart of the issue is a distinction between physical causality—the realm of impersonal events—and moral culpability—the realm of human responsibility.

Little imagination is required to see how the distinction between killing and allowing to die can be challenged. The standard objection encompasses two points. The first is that people can die equally by our omissions as well as our commissions: we can refrain from saving them when it is possible to do so and they will be just as dead as if we shot them. Our decision itself, and not necessarily how we effectuate that decision, is the reason for their death. That fact establishes the basis of the second point: if we *intend* a person's death, it can be brought about as well by acts we omit as by those we commit; the crucial moral point is not how the person dies, but our intention. We can, then, be responsible for the death of another by intending that they die and we accomplish that end by standing aside and allowing them to die.

Despite these criticisms—resting upon ambiguities that can readily be acknowledged—the distinction between killing and allowing to die remains valid. It has not only a logical validity but, no less important, a social validity whose place must be as central in moral judgments about allocation as in individual patient decisions. As a way of elucidating the distinction, I propose that it is best understood as expressing three different, though overlapping, perspectives on nature and human action: metaphysical, moral, and medical.

Metaphysical

The first and most fundamental premise of the distinction between killing and allowing to die is that there is a sharp difference between the self and the external world. Unlike the childish fantasy that the world is nothing more than a projection of the self, or the neurotic person's fear that he or she is responsible for everything that goes wrong, the distinction is meant to uphold a simple notion: there is a world external to the self that has its own, and independent, causal dynamism. A conflation of killing and allowing to die mistakenly assumes that the self has become master of everything within and outside of the self. It is as if the concept that modern humans might ultimately control nature has been internalized, that, if the self might be able to influence nature by its actions, then the self and nature must be one.

But, of course, that is a fantasy. The fact that we can intervene in nature, and cure or control many diseases, does not erase the difference between the self and the external world. It is as "out there" as ever, even if more under our sway. But that sway, however great, is always limited. We can cure disease, but not always the chronic illness that follows the cure. We can forestall death with modern medicine, but death always wins because of the body's inherent limitations, stubbornly beyond final human control. We can distinguish between an aging body and a diseased body, but in the end they always become one and the same body. To attempt to deny the distinction between killing and allowing to die is, then, mistakenly to impute more power to human action than it actually has and to accept the conceit that nature has now fallen wholly within the realm of human control.

Moral

At the center of the distinction between killing and allowing to die is the difference between physical causality and moral culpability. On the one hand, to bring the life of another to an end by an injection is to directly kill the other—our action is the physical cause of death. On the other hand, to allow someone to die from a disease we cannot cure (and that we did not cause) is to permit the *disease* to act as the cause of death. The notion of physical causality in both cases rests on the metaphysical distinction between human agency and the action of external nature. The ambiguity arises precisely because we can be morally culpable of killing someone (unless we have a moral right to do so, as in self-defense) and no less culpable for allowing someone to die (if we have both the possibility and the obligation of keeping that person alive). Thus there are cases where, morally speaking, it makes no difference whether we killed or allowed to die; we are equally responsible morally. In those cases, the lines of physical causality and moral culpability happen to cross. Yet the fact that they can cross *in some cases* in no way shows that they are always, or even usually, one and the same. We can usually dissect the difference in all but the most obscure cases. We should not, then, use the ambiguity of such cases to do away altogether with the distinction between killing and allowing to die. Ambiguity may obscure, but it does not erase the line between the two.

There is one group of ambiguous cases that is especially troublesome. Even if we grant the ordinary validity of the distinction between killing and allowing to die, what about those cases that combine (a) an illness that renders a patient unable to carry out an ordinary biological function (to eat or breathe unassisted, for example), and (b) our decision to turn off a respirator or remove an artificial feeding tube? On the level of physical causality, have we killed the patient or allowed the person to die? In one sense, it is our action that shortens the person's life, and yet in another sense it is the underlying disease that brings that life to an end. I believe it reasonable to say that, since this person's life was being sustained by artificial means (respirator or tube), and that was necessary because of the presence of an incapacitating disease, the disease is the ultimate reality behind the death. Were it not the disease, there would be no need for artificial sustenance in the first place and no moral issue at all. To lose sight of the paramount reality of the disease is to lose sight of the difference between ourselves and the outer world. Our action may hasten, but does not finally cause, this death.

I quickly add, and underscore, a moral point: the person who, without good moral reason, turns off a respirator or pulls a feeding tube, can be morally culpable if there is no good reason to do so. (To cease treatment may or may not be morally acceptable.) The moral question is whether we are obliged to continue treating a life that is being artificially sustained.

There is an analogous issue of importance. Physicians frequently feel morally more responsible for stopping the use of a life-saving device than for not using it in the first place. While the psychology behind that feeling is understandable, there is no significant moral difference between withholding and withdrawing treatment. The point of this now almost universal denial is precisely that an intervention into the disease process does not erase the underlying disease. To accept the fact that a disease cannot be controlled, though an effort was made to do so, is as morally acceptable as deciding in advance that it cannot be successfully controlled.

Medical

The main social purpose of the distinction between killing and allowing to die has been that of protecting the historical role of the physician as one who tries to cure or comfort patients rather than kill them. Physicians have been given special knowledge about the body, knowledge that can be used to kill or to cure. They are also given great privileges in making use of that knowledge. It is thus all the more important that their social role and power be, and be seen to be, a limited power. That power may be used only to cure or comfort, never to kill. Otherwise, it would open the way for powerful misuse and, no less important, represent an intrinsic violation of what it has traditionally meant to be a physician.

Yet if it is possible for physicians to misuse their knowledge and power in order to kill people directly, are they therefore required to use that same knowledge always to keep people alive, always to resist a disease that can kill the patient? The traditional answer has been: not necessarily. For the physician's ultimate obligation is to the welfare of the patient, and excessive treatment can be as detrimental to that welfare as inadequate treatment. Put another way, the obligation to resist the lethal power of disease is limited—it ceases when the patient is unwilling to have it resisted, or when the resistance no longer serves the patient's welfare. Behind this moral premise is the recognition that disease (of some kind) ultimately triumphs, and that death is both inevitable and not always the greatest human evil. To demand of physicians that they always struggle against disease, as if it were always in their power to conquer it, would be to fall into the same metaphysical trap mentioned above: that of assuming that no distinction can be drawn between natural and human agency.

The Allocation Debate

If the implications of doing away with the distinction between killing and allowing to die are momentous for the euthanasia debate and the treatment of individual patients, they are equally grave in their implications for the allocation debate. It is hard, in fact, to see how we can have a reasonable allocation debate without making the distinction central to that debate. Without it, we face a number of stark alternatives. If we cannot morally distinguish between killing and allowing to die, then every allocation decision can be construed as directly killing those who lose out in the process. A refusal to provide life-saving coverage under an entitlement program will be seen as a means of active *involuntary* euthanasia. To allocate money, say, to education rather than to health care could be seen as a decision to kill people for the sake of education (more specifically, to kill the sick to help children).

Given that understanding, health needs would ordinarily trump all other social claims (unless they could be justified also on different grounds); any other choice would be seen as direct killing. I do not invoke here a hypothetical worry. Even now, those who have tried to limit health allocations have been accused by some of using financial arguments as a covert way of ridding society of people unwanted on other grounds, or simply thought too burdensomely expensive to be worth support. Others have been no less quick to complain: for a society to deny health resources to the needy, or to want to limit an entitlement program, is a murderous course, a selfish way to keep for oneself resources that would save the lives of others.

I believe that way of thinking, whether from right or left, is misleading and harmful. To deny the distinction between killing and allowing to die, and then to use that denial as a way of circumventing a necessary debate or decision about allocations, only adds a social error to a metaphysical one. To say this is not to deny that allocation decisions have important life-and-death implications, or that some allocation decisions could be used to mask abominable moral attitudes or practices; or that, in practice, some allocation decisions can be wrong or unfair. I am only trying to say that issues of this kind must be decided on their merits and not dealt with by ignoring or confusing the distinction between killing and allowing to die. That helps nothing.

How, then, can we make difficult allocation decisions in ways that avoid any suggestion that they are being used as a way of wrongly killing people? Or of making them in ways that properly allow us to let disease shorten, or end, life? This problem is all the more complicated for affluent nations. For nations that have nothing, there are only "lifeboat" choices, that is, giving only to one because there is not enough for both. For affluent countries the decision is more complex. We could in this country always spend more on health care. But when would it become unreasonable to do so?

It is not easy to find a moral foothold for making such judgments. They must certainly meet some reasonable tests of justice and fairness, both substantively and procedurally. They ought also to reflect some coherent vision of a good society. I will not take up those important questions here. Instead, I want to focus on the problem of finding the limits of our obligations to others. The Catholic tradition, ordinarily thought to be quite conservative on these matters, has long accepted in principle that the imposition of a grave burden on others is a justifiable reason for a person to choose to forgo life-saving care. An important implication of this principle—though rarely drawn—is that neither society nor families have an obligation to take on excessively heavy financial burdens to save the life of another. We can be asked to do our duty toward one another; we cannot be required to act heroically, or severely to jeopardize the welfare of others for whom we may also be responsible.

This principle, though well established, has been little analyzed, perhaps partly because until recently in most developed countries it has usually been possible for families or society to bear the financial burdens, however heavy.

The needed resources were available. In practice, moreover, it has been a principle that few would be likely to invoke, particularly within the family; though theoretically justifiable, it could *look* selfish, and in application could evoke feelings of great doubt and guilt.

There is another problem about the use of the principle. It is inherently communitarian. It recognizes that the common good of families, or society, can and should on occasion take precedence over individual welfare. That is the kind of principle that Americans at least have been reluctant to embrace. To suggest that individuals may not have an unlimited claim on the assistance of their families or neighbors, or that the latter in turn may have only limited obligations to one another, is a disturbing thought. It has ordinarily been evaded by calls to remove excessive burdens from families and to lay them on the state. Only now, when the resources of the state are being stretched and demands upon it seem to be reaching an intolerable limit, can the principle be considered more openly and directly.

Yet how are we to do so in a responsible, fair, and humane way? We might best approach the problem in stages, working first to minimize financial burdens by voluntary methods and then gradually using more stringent methods.

Voluntary Methods of Choosing Treatment

Some 25–30 percent of Medicare costs, for instance, are incurred by 5 percent or so of its beneficiaries in their last year of life. Almost everyone can think of friends or family members who seem to have received unnecessary treatment in their dying. A long-standing assumption of many is that greater patient choice, particularly in terminal illness, would significantly reduce costs. Yet there is no actual evidence that greater choice would reduce costs. In the Medicare case, the available evidence suggests that behind the high costs lies the difficulty of making a prognosis that death is imminent. Moreover, no one has shown that the costs, though high, are unreasonable or unjust.

There is an even greater difficulty in relying upon voluntary methods to do a decisive job in lowering costs. As the history of the debate over "death with dignity" and allowing to die has shown, it has been exceedingly hard in practice to make termination decisions. Even when there is general agreement that excessive and unwanted care should not be given, disagreements among physicians and family members, uncertainty of prognosis, and fear of legal or moral liability, have made individual decisions troublesome. "Living will" and durable power-of-attorney statutes are certainly desirable for individual welfare, and may be of some economic help. So is ready access to hospice services and facilities. But there is little in the history of such legislation to date to indicate that it can overcome the reluctance of contemporary medicine to declare that anyone is, in fact, dying, and to give up the hope for therapeutic success that is its driving impetus and the greatest source of constantly escalating costs.

Screening for Access to Treatment

A number of experiments and policies have been established in recent years both to evaluate better the efficacy of various treatments and to limit, by preliminary screening, access to therapies that are expensive and unlikely to be helpful to some patients. Second opinions prior to surgery, strict criteria of efficacy for admission to intensive-care units, and development of standards for the use of various diagnostic procedures and treatment therapies, are among the techniques being used. Efforts to evaluate the efficacy of various therapies, while widely commended as a goal, have been pursued only fitfully, especially with respect to the development of standards for the termination of a particular treatment. None of these evaluation, prognosis, and screening methods will be of much economic benefit unless their use becomes mandatory. The increased use of preliminary screening will also have to be matched by methods designed to stop those treatments already underway which are ineffective for a significant prolongation of life.

Useless and Financially Burdensome Treatment

A striking feature of efforts to increase patient choice and to use scientific methods of evaluation and screening, is that they build upon widely accepted values. The appeal to a combination of freedom and science is a powerful one. Their use to promote efficiency and economic savings only enhances their attractiveness. The same cannot be said for taking the next step: that of possibly refusing to continue what some, but not all, would consider useless treatment, and the use of "excessive financial burden" as a reason to deny treatment that might be efficacious. These work directly against the grain. It would seem to many an outrageous denial of freedom to refuse the choice of a treatment when, at least in the eyes of some, that treatment is perfectly valid. It would seem an offense against justice to deny someone a treatment judged medically and scientifically valid on the grounds of its costs, either to a family or to a society.

But these are just the kinds of decisions we may have to make. Let me stalk them by moving through a sequence. When the death of the whole brain was proposed in the late 1960s as the standard for declaring a person dead, there was great resistance. Physicians argued that it should be left to them to make a choice between the traditional definition—spontaneous cessation of heart and lung activity—and the newer definition of brain death. That argument eventually lost. Today brain death is the accepted medical and legal standard. Once a patient has been declared dead by that standard, medical treatment must be stopped; to continue would be to treat a dead body, by definition "useless" treatment. This standard applies even if, in the eyes of his or her family, a patient is by their lights not dead.

Let us take another step. What about the continued treatment of patients in a permanent vegetative state (PVS)?

(PVS is commonly defined as that condition in which higher brain [neocortical] functions have been lost, but the brain stem remains alive.) Should that treatment be considered "useless"? Patients have lived on in this state for years—ten years in the instance of Karen Ann Quinlan and thirty-seven years in another famous case—and there may be ten thousand such patients in the United States today. Recently, various court decisions have upheld the validity of terminating treatment, including artificially provided food and water. But there are many who think that this is nothing more than a form of direct killing, equivalent to active euthanasia. There is just enough scientific uncertainty about diagnosing PVS (or making definite judgments about the state of consciousness of those in that condition) to give these opponents a small degree of medical credibility. Proponents of continued care, moreover, argue that it is a moral, not a medical judgment, to say that a life of permanent unconsciousness is not a life suitable for sustenance. The moral judgment, they claim, should recognize that no one has the right to judge that the life of another is meaningless.

How might one respond to that view? It is not the task of medicine to decide whose life is worth living; that is indeed a moral issue. But it is the task of those who provide care to make prudent judgments concerning treatment that provides no known medical benefits, and, based on present medical knowledge, to determine when someone has lost the capacity for meaningful personal life—at least to the extent that such life requires some minimal level of intact higher brain activity. These judgments may be wrong, but they are not patently irresponsible or indifferent to human life. They are no more and no less than what they claim to be: prudent judgments based on available knowledge.

Those who make such judgments can reasonably conclude that continued treatment of a PVS patient is "useless" and economically indefensible. A family would certainly be justified in claiming that any financial burden imposed upon it was excessive (for the cost of any useless treatment would be excessive); and the society could well claim that it had no obligation to provide expensively useless treatment (Medicaid has most commonly paid the costs of PVS victims).

There has obviously been a great societal reluctance to follow through on such logic. PVS is an ambiguous category because there is a division of opinion, both medical and moral, about whether sustaining patients by artificial feeding is medical treatment, and about whether it is useful or useless. There are those who believe there are neither medical nor solid moral reasons to stop treatment of those in PVS, particularly the provision of food and water (which some do not want to call "treatment" in any case). Theirs may be a minority voice, but it is a strong one. For another, those who believe continued treatment (including food and water) of PVS is unjustified have been willing to support only court decisions pertinent to individual cases in that respect. There have been no concerted efforts to have Medicaid or Medicare deny payment for care of PVS, or to have private insurance carriers do so. It is hard to see how a debate on that reimbursement issue can be forestalled much longer.

Let us take a step to the next category, even more troubling, that of possibly denying the provision of expensive medical treatment that is undeniably efficacious. The most difficult case would be one in which the expensive available treatment is effective and where the prognosis for a full and extended life span is high. This is now the case with kidney, heart, and liver transplants. Since the cost of such transplants is totally beyond the economic capacity of the average family, there has rarely been discussion about families' obligations to take on those costs. Instead, they have resorted either to government support or to public appeals.

Some Boundary Standards

Must we, however, judge that, in an otherwise affluent society, a government decision to refuse to support organ transplantations would be morally unjustifiable? Or to refuse other forms of expensive, efficacious treatment as well? Can a government claim that the provision of some forms of treatment constitutes a grave and excessive burden—which is, in effect, what the state of Oregon has done? No clear answer can be given to a question of this kind, in part because much depends upon particular circumstances. But it is possible, I believe, to fashion some general standards for assessing those circumstances. I will call them boundary standards.

The first such standard is that government cannot automatically be required to pay the costs of whatever new treatments result from scientific advance. Government cannot be held hostage to medical progress, which in the nature of the case is constantly devising new, and often more expensive, treatments and cures. This is an obvious point, but, in practice, it is widely assumed that once a treatment has proved efficacious, government is obliged to pay for it; such has been the history of organ transplantation, as it moved from the experimental to proven therapy. The automatic presumption in favor of reimbursement for whatever treatment has been shown efficacious now must give way to one that is more neutral, that is, one subject to other considerations than progress and proven efficacy.

A second standard is that government cannot be obliged to meet every individual medical need, however valid that need. In an earlier time when medicine was comparatively less effective, there was a relatively uniform range of medical costs. Individual costs of care varied, but only within a relatively narrow range. Medical progress has not only raised the costs of care in general, it has also widened the range of costs. As more can be done to save the lives of individuals, and to save the lives of those afflicted with relatively uncommon conditions or syndromes, the range of spending possibilities broadens. Cases with costs of $500,000 to $1 million become more common; and whole categories, such as neonatal care, increase the discrepancies within individual medical subspecialties. To ask government, in the wake of these developments, to provide individual care regardless of the cost, is to ask too much. That is another way of urging the government to sign blank checks, the amount of which is to be determined by unchecked medical progress as it constantly redefines and expands the concept of "need."

A third standard is that government has the obligation to encompass the full range of human needs, not simply health needs, and to address the entire range of conditions and programs that together make up a coherent society. That is a way of saying that a government would be imprudent, if not irresponsible, to give over a disproportionate share of its resources to meet health-care needs, even if some of those needs are matters of life and death for individuals. Societies need education for their children, police and fire protection, national defense, roads and transportation systems, jobs and economic infrastructures, social welfare programs, and so on. It is a long list.

We can ask what is a proportionate share for each of those categories, and as a society we will argue about that. But there is no reason to exempt the health-care sector from that debate. Government would be well justified, I believe, to say that it cannot allow health claims always to override other social claims, to allow expensive individual health needs to overcome public interest needs (organ transplants over schools), or to allow issues of life and death always to trump issues of social amenities (hospitals over parks).

I offer here no formula for making those hard allocation decisions. But I do want to suggest that, just as we would consider it neurotic and hypochondriacal for an individual to give over an excessive portion of his or her psychic energy and economic resources to the preservation of health, the same is possible for a society. We need to scale down the priority routinely given to health-care needs, and to stand firm in the face of the inevitable medical progress that promises to deliver some benefit, even life itself, to some individuals if only we will collectively pay for it. We need to develop a strong capacity to say no to some of these possibilities. We need to combine an ability to determine limits with sensitive and open public debate about just what it is that makes for a good society, and what is the proper and sensible place to be given to the pursuit of health and the avoidance of death.

Euthanasia

Dan W. Brock

Dan Brock is a professor of philosophy and biomedical ethics at Brown University and directs Brown's Center for Biomedical Ethics. He has long been involved in bioethics and public policy. This article appeared in the *Yale Journal of Biology and Medicine* in 1992.

There is an emerging consensus that competent patients, or the surrogates of incompetent patients, should be permitted to weigh the benefits and burdens of alternative life-sustaining treatments according to the patient's values, and either to refuse any treatment or to select from among available alternative treatments. More recently, significant public and professional attention has shifted from life-sustaining treatment to euthanasia and physician-assisted suicide. Unfortunately, some of the most widely publicized cases, such as those of Dr. Kevorkian, have been sufficiently problematic that even most supporters of euthanasia or physician-assisted suicide did not defend the physicians' actions in them. As a result, the subsequent debate they spawned has often shed more heat than light on the subject. My aim here is to formulate and evaluate some of the central ethical arguments for and against euthanasia. Although my evaluation of the arguments leads me, with reservations, to support permitting euthanasia, my primary aim is to identify confusions in some common arguments, and problematic assumptions and claims that need more defense or data in others. My hope is to advance the debate by focusing attention on what I believe should be the real issues therein.

In the recent bioethics literature, some have endorsed physician-assisted suicide but not euthanasia. Are the two sufficiently different that the moral arguments that apply to one often do not apply to the other? A paradigm case of the former is the provision by a physician of a lethal dose of medication to a patient who asks for it to end his or her life, and who then does so. A paradigm case of euthanasia is a physician him- or herself administering the lethal dose, often when the patient is unable to do so. The only difference that need exist between the two is who actually administers the lethal dose—the physician or the patient. In each instance, the physician plays an active and necessary causal role in providing the lethal dose.

In physician-assisted suicide, the patient acts "last"—for example, in the way Janet Adkins herself pushed the button after Dr. Kevorkian hooked her up to his suicide machine, whereas, in euthanasia, the physician acts "last" by performing the physical equivalent of pushing the button. In both, however, the choice rests fully with the patient. In both, the patient acts "last" in the sense of retaining the right to change his or her mind until the point at which the lethal process becomes irreversible. How could there be a substantial moral difference between them, based only on this small difference in the part played by the physician in the causal process resulting in death? Of course, it might be held that the moral difference is obvious—in euthanasia, the physician kills the patient, whereas, in physician-assisted suicide, the patient kills him- or herself. But this argument is misleading at best. In physician-assisted suicide, the physician and patient together kill the patient, a case of joint action for which both are responsible. I shall take the arguments evaluated below to apply both to physician-assisted suicide and to euthanasia and shall focus on euthanasia.

My concern here will be with *voluntary* euthanasia only; that is, with the case in which a clearly competent patient makes a fully voluntary and persistent request for euthanasia. A last introductory point is that I will examine only secular arguments about euthanasia, though of course many people's attitudes to euthanasia are inextricable from their religious views. I take this secular focus to be appropriate for public policy.

The Central Ethical Argument for Voluntary Active Euthanasia

The central ethical argument for euthanasia is familiar: that the very same two fundamental ethical values that support the consensus on patients' rights to decide about life-sustaining treatment also support the ethical permissibility of euthanasia. These values are individual self-determination or autonomy and individual well-being. By self-determination, as it bears on euthanasia, I mean people's interest in making important decisions about their lives for themselves, according to their own values or conceptions of a good life, and in being left free to act on those decisions. Respecting self-determination permits people to form and to live in accordance with their own conception of a good life and to exercise significant control over their lives. Most people are certainly much concerned about the nature of the last stage of their lives. Death is today increasingly preceded by a long period of significant physical and mental decline, due in part to the technological interventions of modern medicine. For many patients near death, maintaining the quality of one's life, avoiding great suffering, maintaining one's dignity, and ensuring that others remember us as we wish them to, become of paramount importance and outweigh merely extending one's life. Since there is no single, objectively correct answer for everyone, as to when, if at all, when one is critically or terminally ill, one's life becomes (all things considered) a burden and unwanted, the great variance among people on this question makes it especially important that individuals control the manner, circumstances, and timing of their dying and death.

The other main value that supports euthanasia is individual well-being. It might seem that protecting patients' well-being conflicts with a person's self-determination when that person requests euthanasia. Life itself is commonly taken to be a central good for individuals. But when a competent patient decides to forgo all further life-sustaining treatment *or* requests euthanasia, life is no longer considered a benefit by that patient, but has now become a burden. Of course, sometimes there are conditions, such as clinical depression, that call into question whether the patient has made a competent choice, either to forgo life-sustaining treatment or to seek euthanasia, and a determination of incompetence can warrant not honoring the patient's choice.

I emphasize that the value or right of self-determination of patients does not entitle them to compel physicians to act contrary to the physician's own moral or professional values. Physicians are moral and professional agents whose own self-determination or integrity should be respected as well. If performing euthanasia becomes legally permissible, but conflicts with a particular physician's reasonable understanding of his or her moral or professional responsibilities, the care of a patient who requests euthanasia should be transferred to another. But the ethical and policy issue is the permissibility of performing euthanasia by those who do not have moral or professional objections to it.

Opponents of euthanasia commonly offer two types of arguments against euthanasia, which they take to outweigh or to override this support of euthanasia. The first argument is that, in any individual case in which a patient's self-determination and well-being do support euthanasia, it is nevertheless always ethically wrong or impermissible. The second argument grants that, in some individual cases, euthanasia may not be ethically wrong, but maintains nonetheless that ethically sound public and legal policy should never permit it. The first argument focuses on features of any individual case of euthanasia, while the second focuses on a social or legal policy that would permit euthanasia. I will initially consider the first argument.

The Argument That Euthanasia Is Always the Deliberate Killing of an Innocent Person

The claim that any individual instance of euthanasia is a case of deliberate killing of an innocent person is, with only minor qualifications, correct. Unlike forgoing life-sustaining treatment, which is commonly understood as allowing to die, euthanasia is clearly killing. Unlike providing morphine for pain relief at doses where the risk of respiratory depression and an earlier death may be a foreseen but unintended side effect of treating the patient's pain, in euthanasia the patient's death is deliberate or intended, even if in both instances the physician's ultimate end may be to respect the patient's wishes. If there is a sound ethical prohibition of all deliberate killing of an innocent person, euthanasia would be nearly always impermissible, but is such an ethical prohibition defensible?

In the context of medicine, what lends this ethical prohibition plausibility in part is the belief that nothing in the currently accepted practice of medicine is deliberate killing. Thus, according to this view, forgoing of life-sustaining treatment, whether by not starting or by stopping treatment, is allowing the patient to die, not killing, and so is not covered by the ethical prohibition against killing. Common though the view is that stopping life-sustaining treatment is allowing someone to die, I shall argue that the belief is confused and mistaken. Typical cases of stopping life-sustaining treatment are killing; they are not allowing to die, though they are cases of ethically justified killing.

Why is the common view that stopping life-sustaining treatment is allowing to die and not killing a mistaken one? Consider the case of a patient, terminally ill with amyotrophic lateral sclerosis (ALS) disease, who is completely respirator-dependent, with no hope of ever being weaned from the respirator. The patient is unquestionably competent but finds her condition intolerable and persistently requests to be removed from the respirator and allowed to die. Most people would agree that the patient's physician should respect the patient's wishes and remove her from the respirator, though this action will certainly result in the patient's death. The common understanding of what the physician does in removing the patient from the respirator is that the physician thereby allows the patient to die. But is that viewpoint correct?

Suppose the patient has a greedy and hostile son, who mistakenly believes both that his mother will never decide to stop her life-sustaining treatment and that, even if she did, her physician would not remove her from the respirator. Afraid that his inheritance will be dissipated by a long and expensive hospitalization, he enters his mother's room while she is sedated, extubates her, turns off the respirator, and she dies. Shortly thereafter, the medical staff discovers what he has done and confronts the son, who replies, "I didn't kill her; I merely allowed her to die. It was her ALS disease that caused her death." I think this answer would rightly be dismissed as transparent sophistry—the son went into his mother's room and deliberately killed her. But, of course, the son performed just the same physical actions, did just the same thing, that the physician would have done. If that is so, then the physician also kills the patient when he extubates her and stops the respirator.

I underline immediately that there are important ethical differences between what the physician and the greedy son do. First, only the physician acts with the patient's consent. Second, the physician acts with a good motive—to respect the patient's wishes and self-determination—whereas the son acts with a bad motive—to protect his own inheritance. Third, only the physician acts in a social role, in which he is legally authorized to carry out the patient's wishes to stop treatment. These, and perhaps other, ethically important differences show that what the physician did was morally justified, whereas what the son did was morally wrong. What they do *not* show, however, is that the son killed, while the physician allowed to die. One can either kill or allow to die with or without consent, with a good or bad motive, in or not in a social role which legally authorizes one to do so.

Suppose that my argument is mistaken: that stopping life support as well as euthanasia is killing. Euthanasia, though deliberate killing, still need not, for that reason, be morally wrong. To see this point of view, we need to ask: What is it that makes paradigm cases of wrongful killing wrongful? One very plausible answer is that killing denies the victim something that he or she values greatly—continued life or a future. Moreover, since continued life is necessary for pursuing any of a person's plans and purposes, killing brings the frustration of all of these plans and desires as well. In a nutshell, wrongful killing deprives an individual of a valued future and of all that the person wanted and planned to do in that future.

A natural expression of this account of the wrongness of killing is that people have a moral right not to be killed. But in this account of the wrongness of killing, the right not to be killed, like other rights, should be waivable when the individual makes a competent decision that continued life is no longer wanted or a good, but is instead worse than no further life at all. In this rights view of the wrongness of killing, voluntary euthanasia then does not violate that right. I turn now to the evaluation of public policy on euthanasia.

Public Policy: Would the Bad Consequences of Euthanasia Outweigh the Good?

The case against euthanasia at the policy level is stronger than that at the level of evaluation of individual cases, though even here I believe the argument is ultimately unpersuasive, or at best indecisive. There is considerable empirical or factual disagreement about what would be the consequences of a legal policy permitting euthanasia in the United States at this time, which is greatly exacerbated by the highly speculative nature of many of the feared consequences and by the general lack of firm data on the issue.

There is also moral or evaluative disagreement about the relative importance of different good and bad consequences. Despite these difficulties, a preliminary account of the probable main good and bad consequences should help to clarify where better data and/or more moral analysis and argument are needed, as well as where policy safeguards must be developed.

Potential Good Consequences of Permitting Euthanasia

What are the likely good consequences of making euthanasia legally permissible? First, if euthanasia were permitted, it would then be possible to respect the self-determination of competent patients who want it, but now cannot get it because of its illegality. We simply do not know how many such patients and people there are. In the Netherlands, where euthanasia is legally permitted, a recent study estimated that about 2 percent of deaths were from euthanasia or physician-assisted suicide. No straightforward extrapolation to the United States is possible for many reasons, but, even with better data, significant moral disagreement would remain about how much weight or importance should be given to any instance of failure to respect a person's self-determination in this way.

A second good consequence of making euthanasia legally permissible benefits a much larger group. Polls of Americans have shown that a majority of the public believes that people should have a right to obtain euthanasia if they want it. No doubt the vast majority of those who support this right to euthanasia will never in fact come to want it for themselves, but making euthanasia legally permissible would reassure the many who support euthanasia that, if they ever should want it, they would be able to obtain it. The legalization of euthanasia can be thought of as a kind of insurance policy that one will not be forced to endure a protracted dying process that one has come to find burdensome and unwanted, should there be no life-sustaining treatment to forgo.

A third good consequence of the legalization of euthanasia concerns patients whose lives, while they are dying, are filled with severe and unrelievable pain, and for whom euthanasia is the only release from their otherwise prolonged suffering and agony. This argument from mercy has always been the strongest argument for euthanasia in those cases to which it applies. But how often are patients forced to undergo untreatable agony which only euthanasia could relieve? It is crucial to distinguish those patients whose pain *could* be adequately relieved with modern methods of pain control, though in fact it is not, from those whose pain is relievable only by death.

Specialists in pain control—for example, in terminally ill cancer patients—argue that there are very few patients whose pain could not be adequately controlled, though sometimes at the cost of so sedating them that they are effectively unable to interact with other people or their environment. Thus, the argument from mercy in cases of physical pain can probably be met in most cases by providing adequate measures of pain relief, short of euthanasia. This goal should be a high priority, whatever our legal policy on euthanasia. Dying patients often undergo substantial psychological suffering that is not fully or even principally the result of physical pain. If the argument from mercy is extended to patients experiencing great and unrelievable psychological suffering, the numbers of patients to which it applies is much greater.

One last good consequence that proponents of legalizing euthanasia cite is that, once a decision "for death" has been made, it is often more humane to end life quickly and peacefully, as can be done by euthanasia, when that end is what the patient wants. Such a death will often be seen as a better death than a more prolonged one in which the patient may be robbed of his or her dignity.

Some opponents of euthanasia challenge these good consequences of permitting euthanasia, but most opponents of euthanasia cite a number of bad consequences that permitting euthanasia would or could produce.

Potential Bad Consequences of Permitting Euthanasia

I shall first consider an argument specifically against physicians performing euthanasia. The performance of euthanasia by physicians, it is said, would be incompatible with their fundamental moral and professional commitment as healers to care for patients and to protect life. If euthanasia by physicians became common, this sanction would weaken patients' trust in their physicians, as patients came to fear that a medication was intended not to treat or cure, but instead to kill. This position was forcefully stated in a paper by four prominent physicians and bioethicists [in "Doctors Must Not Kill," Part One]:

> The very soul of medicine is on trial. . . . This issue touches medicine at its moral center; if this moral center collapses, if physicians become killers or are even licensed to kill, the profession—and, therewith, each physician—will never again be worthy of trust and respect as healer and comforter and protector of life in all its frailty.

These authors go on to make clear that, while they oppose permitting anyone to perform euthanasia, their special concern is with physicians doing so:

> We call on fellow physicians to say that they will not deliberately kill. We must also say to each of our fellow physicians that we will not tolerate killing of patients and that we shall take disciplinary action against doctors who kill. And we must say to the broader community that if it insists on tolerating or legalizing active euthanasia, it will have to find non-physicians to do its killing.

How persuasive is this claim that permitting physicians to kill would undermine the very "moral center" of medicine? One point is that patients should not fear, as a consequence of *voluntary* active euthanasia becoming permissible, that their physicians will substitute a lethal injection for what patients want and believe is part of their care. If active euthanasia is truly voluntary, then no patient should fear getting it without his or her own voluntary request. Patients' fear of losing control over their care and the circumstances of their dying should be lessened, not strengthened, if euthanasia were permitted, and this policy should strengthen trust in their physicians.

Might these authors, nevertheless, be correct that, if physicians should become killers, the moral center of medicine would collapse? This question raises what, at the deepest level, should be the guiding aims of medicine, a question that obviously cannot be fully explored here. I believe that the two values of respecting patients' self-determination and promoting their well-being should guide physicians' actions as healers, comforters, and protectors of their patients' lives and should be at the "moral center" of medicine. These two values support physicians' performance of euthanasia when their patients make competent requests for it. The proper aims of medicine and the limits on physicians' power will surely be one of the central themes in the continuing debate about euthanasia.

A second possible bad consequence of permitting euthanasia is the weakening of society's commitment to provide optimal care for dying patients. We live at a time in which the control of health care costs has become, and is likely to continue to be, the dominant focus of health care policy. If euthanasia is regarded as a cheaper alternative to adequate care and treatment, then pressure may weaken to ensure that the quality of life of dying patients is appropriately maximized by providing sometimes costly support and other services. Particularly if our society comes to embrace deeper and more explicit rationing of health care, frail, elderly, and dying patients will be in a poor position to be strong and effective advocates for their own health care and other needs.

Here are two reasons for skepticism about this argument. The first is that this same worry could have been directed at recognizing patients' or surrogates' rights to forgo life-sustaining treatment. And yet, there is no persuasive evidence that the gaining by patients and surrogates of rights to forgo life-sustaining treatment caused a serious erosion in the quality of care of dying patients from either a decreased willingness of payers to fund that care or a decreased commitment of professionals or families to provide it. The second reason for skepticism about this worry is that because only a very small proportion of deaths would occur from euthanasia if it were permitted, the vast majority of critically ill and dying patients will still have to be cared for by physicians, families, and others. Permitting euthanasia should not diminish people's commitment and concern to maintain and improve the care of these patients.

The final potential bad consequence of legalizing euthanasia is the central concern of many opponents of euthanasia and, I believe, is the most serious objection to a legal policy permitting euthanasia. According to this "slippery slope" worry, although active euthanasia may be morally permissible in cases in which it is unequivocally voluntary and the patient finds his or her condition unbearable, a legal policy permitting euthanasia would inevitably lead to active euthanasia being performed in many other cases in which it would be morally wrong. In order to prevent those other wrongful cases of euthanasia, we should not permit even morally justified performance of it.

"Slippery slope" arguments of this form are problematic and difficult to evaluate. In this argument's most extreme form, permitting euthanasia is the first and fateful step down the slippery slope to Nazism, a slope that, once we are on, we will be unable to get off. Now it cannot be denied that it is *possible* that permitting euthanasia could have these fateful consequences, but that cannot be enough to warrant prohibiting an otherwise justified practice of euthanasia. A similar *possible* "slippery slope" worry could have been raised over securing competent patients' rights to decide about life support, but recent history shows such a "slippery slope" worry would have been unfounded. How *likely* and *widespread* would be the abuses and unwarranted extensions of permitting euthanasia? Opponents of euthanasia on "slippery slope" grounds have not provided the data or evidence necessary to turn their speculative concerns into well-grounded likelihoods. The character and likelihood of abuses of a legal policy permitting euthanasia depend in significant part on the procedures put in place to protect against them, though there is not space to detail those here. It is possible to reduce substantially, though not to eliminate, the potential for abuse of a policy permitting euthanasia. Any legalization of euthanasia should only be enacted with a well-considered set of procedural safeguards, together with an ongoing process of evaluation of the use of euthanasia.

While I believe necessary distinctions can be made, both in principle and in practice, to largely limit "slippery slope" worries, one legitimate "slippery slope" concern should be acknowledged. There is reason to expect that legalization of voluntary euthanasia might soon be followed by pressure for the legalization of some non-voluntary euthanasia of incompetent patients unable to express their own wishes. Respecting an individual's self-determination and recognizing that continued life is not always a good for someone can support not only voluntary euthanasia, but some non-voluntary euthanasia as well. Recent history with life-sustaining treatment is instructive. There, the right of competent patients has been extended to incompetent patients and exercised by a surrogate, who is to decide as the patient would have decided in the circumstances if competent. It has been plausibly held to be unreasonable to continue life-sustaining treatment that the patient would not have wanted just because the patient now lacks the capacity to tell us so. The very same logic that has extended the right to refuse life-sustaining treatment from a competent patient to the surrogate of an incompetent patient (acting with or without a formal advance directive from the patient) may well do the same in the case of active euthanasia.

This potential for legalization of voluntary euthanasia which in time could be extended to non-voluntary active euthanasia, with surrogates acting for incompetent patients, is the main, legitimate "slippery slope" worry about permitting euthanasia. Even if this practice is a likely outcome, however, its ethical evaluation is more complex than many opponents of euthanasia allow. Just as in the case of surrogates' decisions to forgo life-sustaining treatment for incompetent patients, so also surrogates' decisions for nonvoluntary euthanasia for incompetent persons would often accurately reflect what the incompetent person would have wanted and would deny that person nothing that he or she would have considered a good. If non-voluntary active euthanasia were permitted, however, the potential for misuse and abuse would unquestionably be greater.

Concluding Comments on the Role of Physicians in Euthanasia

If euthanasia is made legally permissible, should physicians take part in it? Should only physicians be permitted to perform it, as is the case in the Netherlands? In discussing above the objection that euthanasia is incompatible with medicine's commitment to curing, caring for, and comforting patients, I argued that it is not incompatible with a proper understanding of the aims of medicine, and so need not undermine patients' trust in their physicians. If so, then physicians probably should not be prohibited, either by law or by professional norms, from taking part in legally permissible euthanasia. Most physicians in the Netherlands appear not to consider euthanasia to be incompatible with their professional commitments.

There are also at least two reasons for restricting any legal permission to perform euthanasia *only* to physicians. First, physicians would inevitably be involved in some of the important procedural safeguards necessary to a defensible practice of euthanasia, such as ensuring that patients are well-informed about their condition, prognosis, and possible treatments, and ensuring that all reasonable means have been taken to improve patients' quality of life. Second, and probably more important, one necessary protection against abuse of any legalization of euthanasia is to limit who is given the authority to perform euthanasia, so that they can be held accountable for their exercise of that authority. That authority could quite reasonably be limited to physicians, whose training and professional norms give some assurance that they would perform euthanasia responsibly.

Death with Dignity
and the Sanctity of Life

Leon R. Kass

Leon R. Kass is one of the four physician-ethicists whose comment on the "Debbie" piece appeared in Part One. He is a professor of humanities at the University of Chicago. In this paper, which was published in *Commentary* in March 1990, Kass sets out his systematic view of the issue.

"Call no man happy until he is dead." With these deliberately paradoxical words, the ancient Athenian sage Solon reminds the self-satisfied Croesus of the perils of fortune and the need to see the end of a life before pronouncing on its happiness. Even the richest man on earth has little control over his fate. The unpredictability of human life is an old story; many a once-flourishing life has ended in years of debility, dependence, and disgrace. But today, it seems, the problems of the ends of lives are more acute, a consequence, ironically, of successful—or partly successful—human efforts to do battle with fortune and, in particular, to roll back medically the causes of death. While many look forward to further triumphs in the war against mortality, others here and now want to exercise greater control over the end of life, by electing death to avoid the burdens of lingering on. The failures resulting from the fight against fate are to be resolved by taking fate still further into our own hands.

This is no joking matter. Nor are the questions it raises academic. They emerge, insistently and urgently, from poignant human situations, occurring daily in hospitals and nursing homes, as patients and families and physicians are compelled to decide matters of life and death, often in the face only of unattractive, even horrible, alternatives. Shall

I allow the doctors to put a feeding tube into my eighty-five-year-old mother, who is unable to swallow as a result of a stroke? Now that it is inserted and she is not recovering, may I have it removed? When would it be right to remove a respirator, forgo renal dialysis, bypass life-saving surgery, or omit giving antibiotics for pneumonia? When in the course of my own progressive dementia will it be right for my children to put me into a home or for me to ask my doctor or my wife or my daughter for a lethal injection? When, if ever, should I as a physician or husband or son accede to—or be forgiven for acceding to— such a request?

These dilemmas can be multiplied indefinitely, and their human significance is hard to capture in words. For one thing, posing them as well defined problems to be solved abstracts from the full human picture, and ignores such matters as the relations between the generations, the meaning of old age, attitudes toward mortality, religious faith, economic resources, and the like. Also, speech does not begin to convey the anguish and heartache felt by those who concretely confront such terrible decisions, nor can it do much to aid and comfort them. No amount of philosophizing is going to substitute for discernment, compassion, courage, sobriety, tact, thoughtfulness, or prudence, all needed on the spot.

Yet the attitudes, sentiments, and judgments of human agents on the spot are influenced, often unwittingly, by speech and opinion, and by the terms in which we formulate our concerns. Some speech may illuminate, other speech may distort; some terms may be more or less appropriate to the matter at hand. About death and dying, once subjects treated with decorous or superstitious silence, there is today an abundance of talk—not to say indecorous chatter. Moreover, this talk frequently proceeds under the aegis of certain increasingly accepted terminologies, which are, in my view, both questionable in themselves and dangerous in their influence. As a result, we are producing a recipe for disaster: urgent difficulties, great human anguish, and high emotions, stirred up with inadequate thinking.

We have no choice but to reflect on our speech and our terminology.

Let me illustrate the power—and the possible mischief—of one notion currently in vogue: the notion of rights. It is now fashionable, in many aspects of public life, to demand what one wants or needs as a matter of rights. How to do the right thing gets translated into a right to get or do your own thing. Thus, roughly two decades ago, faced with the unwelcome fact of excessive medical efforts to forestall death, people asserted and won a right to refuse life-prolonging treatment found to be useless or burdensome. This was, in fact, a reaffirmation of the right to life, liberty, and the pursuit of happiness, even in the face of imminent death. It enabled dying patients to live as they wished, free of unwelcome intrusions, and to let death come when it would. Today, the demand has been raised: we find people asserting a "right to die," grounded not in objective conditions regarding prognosis or the uselessness of treatment, but in the supremacy of choice itself. In the name of choice people claim the right to choose to cease to be choosing beings. From such a right to refuse not only treatment but life itself—from a right to become dead—it is then a small step to the right to be *made* dead: from my right to die will follow your duty to assist me in dying, i.e., to become the agent of my death, if I am not able, or do not wish, to kill myself. And, thanks to our egalitarian tendencies, it will continue to be an easy step to extend all these rights even to those who are incapable of claiming or exercising them for themselves, with proxies empowered to exercise a right to demand death for the comatose. No one bothers very much about where these putative rights come from or what makes them right, and simple reflection will show that many of them are incoherent.

Comparable mischief can, of course, be done beginning with the notion of duty. From the acknowledged human duty not to shed innocent blood follows the public duty to protect life against those who would threaten it. This gets extended to a duty to preserve life in the face of disease or other non-human dangers to life. This gets extended to a duty to prolong life whenever possible, regardless of the condition of that life or the wishes of its bearer. This gets extended to an unconditional duty never to let death happen, if it is in one's power to do so. This position, sometimes alleged—I think mistakenly—to be entailed by belief in the "sanctity of life," could even make obligatory a search for the conquest of death altogether, through research on aging. Do we have such duties? On what do they rest? And can such a duty to prevent death—or a right to life—be squared with a right to be made dead? Is not this intransigent language of rights and duties unsuitable for finding the best course of action, in these terribly ambiguous and weighty matters? We must try to become more thoughtful about the terms we use and the questions we pose.

Toward this end I wish to explore here the relation between two other powerful notions, both prominent in the discussions regarding the end of life: death with dignity, and the sanctity of life. Both convey elevated, indeed lofty, ideas: what, after all, could be higher than human dignity, unless it were something sacred? As a result, each phrase often functions as a slogan or a rallying cry, though seldom with any regard for its meaning or ground. In the current debates about euthanasia, we are often told that these notions pull in opposite directions. Upholding death with dignity might mean taking actions that would seem to deny the sanctity of life. Conversely, unswervingly upholding the sanctity of life might mean denying to some a dignified death. This implied opposition is, for many of us, very disquieting. The dilemmas themselves are bad enough. Much worse is it to contemplate that human dignity and sanctity might be opposed, and that we may be forced to choose between them.

The confrontation between upholders of death with dignity and upholders of the sanctity of life is in fact nothing new. Two decades ago, the contest was over termination of treatment and letting die. Today and tomorrow, the issue is and will be assisted suicide, mercy killing, so-called active euthanasia. On the extremes stand the same opponents, many of whom—I think mistakenly—think the issues are the same. Many who now oppose mercy killing or voluntary euthanasia then opposed termination of treatment, thinking it equivalent to killing. Those who today back mercy killing in fact agree: if it is permissible to choose death by letting die, they argue, why not also by active steps to hasten, humanely, the desired death? Failing to distinguish between letting die and making dead (by failing to distinguish between intentions and deeds, causes and results, goals and outcomes), both sides polarize the debate, opposing not only one another but also those in the uncomfortable middle. For them, it is *either* sanctity of life *or* death with dignity: one must choose.

I do not accept this polarization. Indeed, in the rest of this essay I mean to suggest the following. First, human dignity and the sanctity of life are not only compatible, but, if rightly understood, go hand in hand. Second, death with dignity, rightly understood, has largely to do with exercising the humanity that life makes possible, often to the very end, and very little to do with medical procedures or the causes of death. Third, the sanctity-and-dignity of life is entirely compatible with letting die but not with deliberately killing. Finally, the practice of euthanasia will not promote human dignity, and our rush to embrace it will in fact only accelerate the various tendencies in our society that undermine not only dignified conduct but even decent human relations.

The Sanctity of Life (and Human Dignity)

What exactly is meant by the sanctity of life? This turns out to be difficult to say. In the strictest sense, sanctity of life would mean that life is *in itself* something holy or sacred, transcendent, set apart—like God Himself. Or, again, focusing on our responses to the sacred, it would mean that life is something before which we stand (or should stand) with reverence, awe, and grave respect—because it is beyond us and unfathomable. In more modest but also more practical terms, to regard life as sacred means that it should not be violated, opposed, or destroyed and, positively, that it should be protected, defended, and preserved. Despite their differences, these various formulations agree in this: that "sacredness," whatever it is, inheres in life itself, and that life, *by its very being*, calls forth an appropriate human response, whether of veneration or restraint. To say that sacredness is something that can be conferred or ascribed—or removed—by solely human agreement or decision is to miss the point entirely.

I have made a modest and so far unsuccessful effort to trace the origin of the sanctity-of-life doctrine in our own Judeo-Christian traditions. To the best of my knowledge, the phrase "sanctity of life" does not occur either in the Hebrew Bible or in the New Testament. Life as such is not said to be holy (qâdosh), as is, for example, the Sabbath. The Jewish people are said to be a holy people, and they are enjoined to be holy as God is holy. True, traditional Judaism places great emphasis on preserving human life—even the holy Sabbath may be violated to save a life, implying to some that a human life is more to be revered than the Sabbath—yet the duty to preserve one's life is not unconditional: to cite only one example, a Jew should accept martyrdom rather than commit idolatry, adultery, or murder.

As murder is the most direct assault on human life and the most explicit denial of its sanctity, perhaps we gain some access to the meaning of the sanctity of life by thinking about why murder is proscribed. If we could uncover the ground of restraint against murder, perhaps we could learn something of the nature of the sanctity of life, and, perhaps, too, of its relation to human dignity. As a result, we might be in a better position to consider the propriety of letting die, of euthanasia, and of other activities advocated by the adherents of "death with dignity."

Why is killing another human being wrong? Can the prospective victim's request to be killed nullify the wrongness of such killing, or, what is more, make such killing right? Alternatively, are there specifiable states or conditions of a human being's life that would justify—or excuse—someone else's directly and intentionally making him dead, even *without* request? The first question asks about murder, the second and third ask whether assisting suicide and mercy killing (so-called active euthanasia) can and should be morally distinguished from murder. The answers regarding assisting suicide and euthanasia will depend on the answer regarding murder, that is, on the *reasons* it is wrong.

Why is murder wrong? The laws against murder are, of course, socially useful. Though murders still occur, despite the proscriptive law and the threat of punishment, civil society is possible only because people generally accept and abide by the reasonableness of this rule. In exchange for society's protection of one's own life against those who might otherwise take it away, each member of society sacrifices, in principle, his (natural) right to the lives of all others. Civil society requires peace, and civil peace depends absolutely on the widespread adherence to the maxim, "Thou shalt not murder." This usefulness of the taboo against murder is sometimes offered as the basis of its goodness: killing is bad because it makes life unsafe and society impossible.

But this alone cannot account for the taboo against murder. In fact, the goodness of civil society is itself predicated upon the goodness of human life, which society is instituted to defend and foster. Civil society exists to defend the goods implicit in the taboo against murder, at least as much as the taboo against murder is useful in preserving civil society.

However valuable any life may be to society, each life is primarily and preeminently valued by the person whose life it is. Individuals strive to stay alive, both consciously and unconsciously. The living body, quite on its own, bends every effort to maintain its living existence. The built-in impulses toward self-preservation and individual well-being that penetrate our consciousness, say, as hunger or fear of death, are manifestations of a deep-seated and powerful will-to-live. These thoughts might suggest that murder is wrong because it opposes this will-to-live, because it deprives another of life against his will, because it kills someone who does not *want* to die. This sort of reason would explain why suicide—self-willed self-killing—might be right, while murder—killing an innocent person against his will—would always be wrong.

Let us consider this view more closely. Certainly, there are some invasions or "violations" of another's body that are made innocent by consent. Blows struck in a boxing match or on the football field do not constitute assault; conversely, an unwelcome kiss from a stranger, because it is an unconsented touching, constitutes a battery, actionable at law. In these cases, the willingness or unwillingness of the "victim" alone determines the rightness or wrongness of the bodily blows. Similar arguments are today used to explain the wrongness of rape: it is "against our wills," a violation not (as we once thought) of womanliness or chastity or nature but of freedom, autonomy, personal self-determination. If consent excuses—or even justifies—these "attacks" on the body of another, might not consent excuse—or justify—the ultimate, i.e., lethal, attack, turning murder into mere (unwrongful) homicide? A person can be murdered only if he personally does not want to be dead.

There is something obviously troublesome about this way of thinking about crimes against persons. Indeed, the most abominable practices, proscribed in virtually all societies, are *not* excused by consent. Incest, even between consenting adults, is still incest; cannibalism would not become merely *delicatessen* if the victim freely gave permission; ownership of human beings, voluntarily accepted, would still be slavery. The violation of the other is independent of the state of the will (in fact, both of victim and perpetrator).

The question can be put this way: is the life of another human being to be respected only because that person (or society) *deems* or *wills* it respectable, or is it to be respected because it *is in itself* respectable? If the former, then human worth depends solely on agreement or human will; since will confers dignity, will can take it away, and a permission to violate nullifies the violation. If the latter, then one can never be freed from the obligation to respect human life by a request to do so, say, from someone who no longer values his own life.

This latter view squares best with our intuitions. We are not entitled to dismember the corpse of a suicide nor may we kill innocently those consumed by self-hatred. According to our law, killing the willing, the unwilling, and the nonwilling (e.g., infants, the comatose) are all equally murder. Beneath the human will, indeed, the *ground* of human will, is something that commands respect and restraint, willy-nilly. We are to abstain from killing because of something respectable about human beings as such. But what is it?

In Western societies, moral notions trace back to biblical religion. The bedrock of Jewish and Christian morality is the Ten Commandments. "Thou shalt not murder"—the sixth commandment—heads up the so-called second table, which enunciates (negatively) duties toward one's fellow man. From this fact, some people have argued that murder is wrong solely because God said so. After all, that He had to legislate against it might imply that human beings on their own did not know that it was bad or wrong. And even were they to intuit *that* murder is wrong, they might never be able to answer, if challenged, *why* it is wrong; this human inability to supply the reason would threaten the power of the taboo. Thus, so the argument goes, God's will supplies the missing reason for the human rule.

This argument is not satisfactory. True, divine authority elevates the standing and force of the commandments. But it does not follow that they "make sense" only because God willed them. Pagans yesterday believed and atheists today still believe that murder is wrong. In fact, the entire second table of the Decalogue is said to propound not so much divine law as natural law, law suitable for man as man, not only for Jew or Christian.

The Bible itself provides evidence in support of this interpretation, at least about murder. In reporting the first murder, committed by Cain upon his brother Abel before there was any given or known law against it, Abel's blood is said to cry out from the earth in protest against his brother's deed. (The crime, it seems, was a crime against blood and life, not against will, human or divine.) And Cain's denial of knowledge ("Am I my brother's keeper?") seems a clear indication of guilt: if there were nothing wrong with murder, why hide one's responsibility? A "proto-religious" dread accompanies the encounter with death, especially violent death.

But the best evidence comes shortly afterward, in the story of the covenant with Noah: the first law against murder is explicitly promulgated for all mankind united, well before there are Jews or Christians or Muslims. This passage is worth looking at in some detail because, unlike the enunciation of the sixth commandment, it offers a specific reason why murder is wrong.

The prohibition of murder is part of the new order following the Flood. Before the Flood, human beings lived in the absence of law or civil society. The result appears to be something like what Hobbes called the state of nature characterized as a condition of war of each against all. Might alone makes right, and no one is safe. The Flood washes out human life in its natural state; immediately after the Flood, some form of law and justice is instituted, and nascent civil society is founded.

At the forefront of the new order is a newly articulated respect for human life, expressed in the announcement of the punishment for homicide:

> Whoso sheddeth man's blood, by man shall his blood be shed; for in the image of God made He man. *(Genesis 9:6)*

Like law in general, this cardinal law combines speech and force. The threat of capital punishment stands as a deterrent to murder and hence provides a motive for obedience. But the measure of the punishment is instructive. By equat-

ing a life for a life—*no more* than a life for a life, and the
life only of the murderer, not also of his wife and children—
the threatened punishment implicitly teaches the *equal*
worth of each human life. Such equality can be grounded
only in the equal *humanity* of each human being. Against
our own native self-preference, and against our tendency to
overvalue what is our own, blood-for-blood conveys the
message of universality and equality.

But murder is to be avoided not only to avoid the punishment. That may be a motive, which speaks to our fears;
but there is also a reason, which speaks to our minds and
our loftier sentiments. The fundamental reason that makes
murder wrong— and that even justifies punishing it homi-
cidally!—is man's divine-like status. Not the other fellow's
unwillingness to be killed, not even (or only) our desire to
avoid sharing his fate, but *his*—any man's—*very being* requires that we respect his life. Human life is to be respected
more than animal life, because man is more than an animal; man is said to be god-like. Please note that the *truth*
of the Bible's assertion does *not* rest on biblical authority:
man's more-than-animal status is in fact performatively
proved whenever human beings quit the state of nature and
set up life under such a law. The law which establishes that
men are to be law-abiding both insists on, and thereby
demonstrates the truth of, the superiority of man.

How is man God-like? Genesis 1—where it is first said
that man is created in God's image—introduces us to the
divine *activities* and *powers*: (1) God speaks, commands,
names, and blesses; (2) God makes and makes freely; (3)
God looks at and beholds the world; (4) God is concerned
with the goodness or perfection of things; (5) God addresses solicitously other living creatures. In short: God
exercises speech and reason, freedom in doing and making,
and the powers of contemplation, judgment, and care.

Doubters may wonder whether this is truly the case about
God—after all, it is only on biblical authority that we regard God as possessing these powers and activities. But it is
certain that we human beings have them, and that they lift

us above the plane of a merely animal existence. Human beings, alone among the earthly creatures, speak, plan, create, contemplate, and judge. Human beings, alone among the creatures, can articulate a future goal and bring it into being by their own purposive conduct. Human beings, alone among the creatures, can think about the whole, marvel at its articulated order, and feel awe in beholding its grandeur and in pondering the mystery of its source.

A complementary, preeminently moral, gloss on the "image of God" is provided—quite explicitly—in Genesis 3, at the end of the so-called second creation story:

> Now the man is become *like one of us* knowing good and bad. . . . (3:22; emphasis added)

Human beings, unlike the other animals, distinguish good and bad, have opinions and care about their difference, and constitute their whole life in the light of this distinction. Animals may suffer good and bad, but they have no notion of either. Indeed, the very pronouncement, "Murder is bad," constitutes proof of *this* god-like quality of human beings.

In sum, man has special standing because he shares in reason, freedom, judgment, and moral concern, and, as a result, lives a life freighted with moral self-consciousness. Speech and freedom are used, among other things, to promulgate moral rules and to pass moral judgments, first among which is that murder is to be punished in kind because it violates the dignity of such a moral being. We note a crucial implication. To put it simply: the *sanctity* of human life rests absolutely on the *dignity*—the god-likeness—of human beings.

Yet man is, at most, only god*ly*; he is not God or a god. To be an image is also to be *different* from that of which one is an image. Man is, at most, a *mere* likeness of God. With us, the seemingly godly powers and concerns described above occur conjoined with our animality. We are also flesh and blood—no less than the other animals. God's image is tied to blood, which is the life.

The point is crucial, and stands apart from the text that teaches it: everything high about human life—thinking, judging, loving, willing, acting—depends absolutely on everything low—metabolism, digestion, respiration, circulation, excretion. In the case of human beings, "divinity" needs blood—or "mere" life—to sustain itself. And because of what it holds up, human blood—that is, human life— deserves special respect, beyond what is owed to life as such: the low ceases to be the low. (Modern physiological evidence could be adduced in support of this thesis: in human beings, posture, gestalt, respiration, sexuality, and fetal and infant development, among other things, all show the marks of the co-presence of rationality.) The biblical text elegantly mirrors this truth about its subject, subtly merging both high and low: though the *reason* given for punishing murder concerns man's *godliness*, the *injunction* itself concerns man's *blood*. Respect the god-like; do not shed its blood! Respect for anything *human* requires respecting *everything* human, requires respecting *human being* as such.

We have found, I believe, what we were searching for: a reason immanent in the nature of things for finding fault with taking human life, apart from the needs of society or the will of the victim. The wanton spilling of human blood is a violation and a desecration, not only of our laws and wills but of being itself.

We have also found the ground for repudiating the opposition between the sanctity of life and human dignity. Each rests on the other. Or, rather, they are mutually implicated, as inseparable as the concave and the convex. Those who seek to pull them apart are, I submit, also engaged in wanton, albeit intellectual, violence.

Unfortunately, the matter cannot simply rest here. Though the principle seems well established, there is a difficulty, raised in fact by the text itself. How can one assert the inviolability of human life and, in the same breath, insist that human beings deliberately *take* human life to punish those who shed human blood? There are, it seems, sometimes good reasons for shedding human blood, notwithstanding that man is in God's image. We have admitted the dangerous principle: humanity, to uphold the dignity of the human, must sometimes shed human blood.

Bringing this new principle to the case of euthanasia, we face the following challenge to the prior, and more fundamental, principle, shed no human blood: what are we to think when the continuing circulation of human blood no longer holds up anything very high, when it holds up little more—or even *no* more—than metabolism, digestion, respiration, circulation, and excretion? What if human godliness appears to be humiliated by the degradation of Alzheimer's disease or paraplegia or rampant malignancy? And what if it is the well-considered aspiration of the "godlike" to put an end to the humiliation of that very godliness, to halt the mockery that various severe debilities make of a *human* life? Are there here to be found other exceptions to our rule against murder, in which the dignity of a human life can (only?) be respected by ending it?

The first thing to observe, of course, is that the cases of euthanasia (or suicide) and capital punishment are vastly different. One cannot by an act of euthanasia deter or correct or obtain justice from the "violator" of human dignity; senility and terminal illness are of natural origin and can be blamed on no human agent. To be precise, these evils may in their result undermine human dignity, but, lacking malevolent intention, cannot be said to insult it or deny it. They are reasons for sadness, not in*dign*ation, unless one believes, as the tyrant does, that the cosmos owes him good and not evil and exists to satisfy his every wish. Moreover, one does not come to the defense of diminished human dignity by finishing the job, by annihilating the victims. Human dignity would be no more vindicated by euthanizing patients with Alzheimer's disease than it would be by executing as polluted the victims of rape.

Nevertheless, the question persists, and an affirmative

answer remains the point of departure for the active euthanasia movement. Many who fly the banner of "death with
dignity" insist that it centrally includes the option of active
euthanasia, especially when requested. In order to respond
more adequately to this challenge, we need first a more
careful inquiry into "death with dignity."

Death with Dignity

The phrase "death with dignity," whatever it means precisely, certainly implies that there are more and less dignified ways to die. The demand for death with dignity arises
only because more and more people are encountering in
others and fearing for themselves or their loved ones the
deaths of the less dignified sort. This point is indisputable.
The possibility of dying with dignity can be diminished or
undermined by many things, for example, by coma or senility or madness, by unbearable pain or extensive paralysis, by isolation, by institutionalization or destitution, by
sudden death, as well as by excessive or impersonal medical
interventions directed toward the postponement of death. It
is the impediments connected with modern medicine that
increasingly arouse indignation, and the demand for death
with dignity pleads for the removal of these "unnatural"
obstacles.

More generally, the demand for autonomy and the cry for
dignity are asserted against a medicalization and institutionalization of the end of life that robs the old and the
incurable of most of their autonomy and dignity: intubated
and electrified with bizarre mechanical companions, confined and immobile, helpless and regimented, once proud
and independent people find themselves cast in the roles of
passive, obedient, highly disciplined children. Death with
dignity means, in the first instance, the removal of these
added indignities and dehumanizations of the end of life.

One can only sympathize with this concern. Yet even if
successful, efforts to remove these obstacles would not yet
produce a death with dignity. For one thing, not all obsta-

cles to dignity are artificial and externally imposed. Infirmity and incompetence, dementia and immobility—all of them of natural origins—greatly limit human possibility, and for many of us they will be sooner or later unavoidable, the products of inevitable bodily or mental decay. Second, there is nothing of human dignity in the process of dying itself—only in the way we face it: at its best, death with complete dignity will always be compromised by the extinction of dignified humanity; it is, I suspect, a death-denying culture's anger about dying and mortality that expresses itself in the partly oxymoronic and unreasonable demand for dignity in death. Third, insofar as we seek better health and longer life, insofar as we turn to doctors to help us get better, we necessarily and voluntarily compromise our dignity: being a patient rather than an agent is, humanly speaking, undignified. All people, especially the old, willingly, if unknowingly, accept a whole stable of indignities simply by seeking medical assistance. The really proud people refuse altogether to submit to doctors and hospitals. It is well to be reminded of these limits on our ability to roll back the indignities that assault the dying, so that we might acquire more realistic expectations about just how much dignity a "death-with-dignity" campaign can provide.

A death with positive dignity—which may turn out to be something rare, like a life with dignity—entails more than the absence of external indignities. Dignity in the face of death cannot be given or conferred from the outside but requires a dignity of soul in the human being who faces it. To understand the meaning of and prospects for death with dignity, we need first to think more about dignity itself, what it is.

Dignity is, to begin with, an undemocratic idea. The central notion, etymologically, both in English and in its Latin root *(dignitas)*, is that of worthiness, elevation, honor, nobility, height—in short, of excellence or virtue. In all its meanings it is a term of distinction; dignity is not something which, like a nose or a navel, is to be expected or found in every living human being. Dignity is, in principle, aristocratic.

It follows that dignity, thus understood, cannot be demanded or claimed; for it cannot be provided and it is not owed. One has no more *right* to dignity—and hence to dignity in death—than one has to beauty or courage or wisdom, desirable though these all may be.

One can, of course, seek to democratize the principle; one can argue that "excellence," "being worthy," is a property of all human beings, say, for example, in comparison with animals or plants, or with machines. This, I take it, is what is often meant by "*human* dignity." This is also what is implied when one asserts that much of the terminal treatment of dying patients is dehumanizing, or that attachments to catheters, respirators, and suction tubes hide the human countenance and thereby insult the dignity of the dying. I myself earlier argued that the special dignity of the human species, thus understood, is the ground of the sanctity of human life. Yet on further examination this universal attribution of dignity to human beings pays tribute more to human potentiality, to the *possibilities* for human excellence. *Full* dignity, or dignity properly so-called, would depend on the *realization* of these possibilities. *Among* human beings, there would still be, on any such material principle, distinctions to be made. If universal human dignity is grounded, for example, in the moral life, in that everyone faces and makes moral choices, dignity would seem to depend mainly on having a *good* moral life, that is, on choosing well. Is there not more dignity in the courageous than in the cowardly, in the moderate than in the self-indulgent, in the righteous than in the wicked?

But courage, moderation, righteousness, and the other human virtues are not solely confined to the few. Many of us strive for them, with partial success, and still more of us do ourselves honor when we recognize and admire those people nobler and finer than ourselves. With proper models, proper rearing, and proper encouragement, many of us can be and act more in accord with our higher natures. In these ways, the openness to dignity can perhaps be democratized still further.

In truth, if we know how to look, we find evidence of human dignity all around us, in the valiant efforts ordinary people make to meet necessity, to combat adversity and disappointment, to provide for their children, to care for their parents, to help their neighbors, to serve their country. Life provides numerous hard occasions that call for endurance and equanimity, generosity and kindness, courage and self-command. Adversity sometimes brings out the best in a man, and often shows best what he is made of. Confronting our own death—or the deaths of our beloved ones—provides an opportunity for the exercise of our humility, for the great and small alike. Death with dignity, in its most important sense, would mean a dignified attitude and virtuous conduct in the face of death.

What would such a dignified facing of death require? First of all, it would require knowing that one is dying. One cannot attempt to settle accounts, make arrangements, complete projects, keep promises, or say farewell if one does not know the score. Second, it requires that one remain to some degree an agent rather than (just) a patient. One cannot make a good end of one's life if one is buffeted about by forces beyond one's control, if one is denied a decisive share in decisions about medical treatments, institutionalization, and the way to spend one's remaining time. Third, it requires the upkeep—as much as possible—of one's familial, social, and professional relationships and activities. One cannot function as an actor if one has been swept off the stage and been abandoned by the rest of the cast. It would also seem to require some direct, self-conscious confrontation, in the loneliness of one's soul, with the brute fact and meaning of nearing one's end. Even, or especially, as he must be passive to the forces of decay, the dignified human being can preserve and reaffirm his humanity by seeing clearly and without illusion. (It is for this reason, among others, that sudden and unexpected death, however painless, robs a man of the opportunity to have a dignified end.)

But as a dignified human life is not just a lonely project against an inevitable death, but a life whose meaning is entwined in human relationships, we must stress again the importance for a death with dignity—as for a life with dignity—of dignified human intercourse with all those around us. Who we are to ourselves is largely inseparable from who we are to and for others; thus, our own exercise of dignified humanity will depend crucially on continuing to receive respectful treatment from others. The manner in which we are addressed, what is said to us or in our presence, how our bodies are tended or our feelings regarded —in all these ways, our dignity in dying can be nourished and sustained. Dying people are all too easily reduced ahead of time to "thinghood" by those who cannot bear to deal with the suffering or disability of those they love. Objectification and detachment are understandable defenses. Yet this withdrawal of contact, affection, and care is probably the greatest single cause of the dehumanization of dying. Death with dignity requires absolutely that the survivors treat the human being at all times as if full god-likeness remains, up to the very end.

It will, I hope, now be perfectly clear that death with dignity, understood as living dignifiedly in the face of death, is not a matter of pulling plugs or taking poison. To speak this way—and it is unfortunately common to speak this way—is to shrink still further the notion of human dignity, and thus heap still greater indignity upon the dying, beyond all the insults of illness and the medicalized bureaucratization of the end of life. If it really is death with dignity we are after, we must think in human and not technical terms. With these thoughts firmly in mind, we can turn in closing back to the matter of euthanasia.

Euthanasia: Undignified and Dangerous

Having followed the argument to this point, even a friendly reader might chide me as follows: "Well and good to think humanistically, but tough practical dilemmas arise, precisely about the use of techniques, and they must be addressed. Not everyone is so fortunate as to be able to die at home, in the company of a loving family, beyond the long reach of the medical-industrial complex. How should these technical decisions—about respirators and antibiotics and feeding tubes and, yes, even poison—be made, precisely in order to uphold human dignity and the sanctity of life that you say are so intermingled?" A fair question: I offer the following outline of an answer.

About treatment for the actually dying, there is in principle no difficulty. In my book, *Toward a More Natural Science*, I have argued for the primacy of easing pain and suffering, along with supporting and comforting speech, and, more to the point, the need to draw back from some efforts at prolongation of life that prolong or increase only the patient's pain, discomfort, and suffering. Although I am mindful of the dangers and aware of the impossibility of writing explicit rules for ceasing treatment—hence the need for prudence—considerations of the individual's health, activity, and state of mind must enter into decisions of *whether* and *how vigorously* to treat if the decision is indeed to be for the patient's good. Ceasing treatment and allowing death to occur when (and if) it will, can, under some circumstances, be quite compatible with the respect that life itself commands for itself. For life can be revered not only in its preservation, but also in the manner in which we allow a given life to reach its terminus.

What about so-called active euthanasia, the direct making dead of someone who is not yet dying or not dying "fast enough"? Elsewhere I have argued at great length against the practice of euthanasia *by physicians*, partly on the grounds of bad social consequences, but mainly on the grounds that killing patients—even those who ask for death—violates the inner meaning of the art of healing. Powerful prudential arguments—unanswerable, in my view—have been advanced as to why legalized mercy killing would be a disastrous social policy, at least for the United States. But some will insist that social policy cannot remain deaf to cries for human dignity, and that dangers must be run to preserve a dignified death through euthanasia, at least where it is requested. As our theme here is dignity and sanctity, I will confine my answer to the question of euthanasia and human dignity.

Let us begin with voluntary euthanasia—the request for assistance in dying. To repeat: the claim here is that the choice for death, because a free act, affirms the dignity of free will against dumb necessity. Or, using my earlier formulation, is it not precisely dignified for the "god-like" to put a voluntary end to the humiliation of that very godliness?

In response, let me start with the following questions. Do the people who are actually contemplating euthanasia *for themselves*—as opposed to their proxies who lead the euthanasia movement—generally put their requests in these terms? Or are they not rather looking for a way to end their troubles and pains? One can *sympathize* with such a motive, out of compassion, but can one admire it, out of respect? Is it really *dignified* to seek to escape from troubles for oneself? Is there, to repeat, not more dignity in courage than in its absence?

Euthanasia for one's own dignity is, at best, paradoxical, even self-contradictory: how can I honor myself by making myself nothing? Even if dignity were to consist solely in autonomy, is it not an embarrassment to claim that autonomy reaches its zenith precisely as it disappears? Voluntary euthanasia, in the name of *positive* dignity, does not make sense.

Acknowledging the paradox, some will still argue the cause of freedom on a more narrow ground: the prospect of euthanasia increases human freedom by increasing options. It is, of course, a long theoretical question whether human freedom is best understood—and best served—through the increase of possibilities. But as a practical matter, in the *present* case, I am certain that this view is mistaken. On the contrary, the opening up of this "option" of assisted suicide will greatly constrain human choice. For the choice for death is not one option among many, but an option to end all options. Socially, there will be great pressure on the aged and the vulnerable to exercise this option. Once there looms the legal alternative of euthanasia, it will plague and burden every decision made by any seriously ill elderly person—not to speak of their more powerful caretakers— even without the subtle hints and pressures applied to them by others.

And, thinking about others, is it dignified to ask or demand that someone else become my killer? It may be sad that one is unable to end one's own life, but can it conduce to either party's dignity to make the request? Consider its double meaning if made to a son or daughter: Do you love me so little as to force me to live on? Do you love me so little as to want me dead? What person in full possession of his own dignity would inflict such a duty on anyone he loved?

Of course, the whole thing could be made impersonal. No requests to family members, only to physicians. But precisely the same point applies: how can one demand care and humanity from one's physician, and, at the same time, demand that he play the role of technical dispenser of death? To turn the matter over to nonphysicians, that is, to technically competent professional euthanizers, is, of course, completely to dehumanize the matter.

Proponents of euthanasia do not understand human dignity, which, at best, they confuse with humaneness. One of their favorite arguments proves this point: why, they say, do we put animals out of their misery but insist on compelling fellow human beings to suffer to the bitter end? Why, if it is not a contradiction for the veterinarian, does the medical ethic absolutely rule out mercy killing? Is this not simply inhumane?

Perhaps inhumane, but not thereby inhuman. On the

contrary, it is precisely because animals are not human that we must treat them (merely) humanely. We put dumb animals to sleep because they do not know that they are dying, because they can make nothing of their misery or mortality, and, therefore, because they cannot live deliberately—i.e., humanly—in the face of their own suffering or dying. They cannot live out a fitting end. Compassion for their weakness and dumbness is our only appropriate emotion, and given our responsibility for their care and well-being, we do the only humane thing we can. But when a conscious human being asks us for death, by that very action he displays the presence of something that precludes our regarding him as a dumb animal. Humanity is owed humanity, not humaneness. Humanity is owed the bolstering of the human, even or especially in its dying moments, in resistance to the temptation to ignore its presence in the sight of suffering.

What humanity needs most in the face of evils is courage, the ability to stand against fear and pain and thoughts of nothingness. The deaths we most admire are those of people who, knowing that they are dying, face the fact frontally and act accordingly: they set their affairs in order, they arrange what could be final meetings with their loved ones, and yet, with strength of soul and a small reservoir of hope, they continue to live and work and love as much as they can for as long as they can. Because such conclusions of life require courage, they call for our encouragement—and for the many small speeches and deeds that shore up the human spirit against despair and defeat.

And what of non-voluntary euthanasia, for those too disabled to request it for themselves—the comatose, the senile, the psychotic: can this be said to be in the service of *their* human dignity? If dignity is, as the autonomy people say, tied crucially to consciousness and will, non-voluntary or "proxy-voluntary" euthanasia can never be a dignified act for the one euthanized. Indeed, it is precisely the absence of dignified humanity that invites the thought of active euthanasia in the first place.

Is it really true that such people are beneath all human dignity? I suppose it depends on the particulars. Many people in greatly reduced states still retain clear, even if partial, participation in human relations. They may respond to kind words or familiar music, they may keep up pride in their appearance or in the achievements of the grandchildren; they may take pleasure in reminiscences or simply in having someone who cares enough to be present; conversely, they may be irritated or hurt or sad, even appropriately so; and, even nearer bottom, they may be able to return a smile or a glance in response to a drink of water or a change of bedding or a bath. Because we really do not know their inner life—what they feel and understand—we run the risk of robbing them of opportunities for dignity by treating them as if they had none. It does not follow from the fact that *we* would never willingly trade places with them that *they* have *nothing* left worth respecting.

But what, finally, about the very bottom of the line, say, people in a "persistent vegetative state," unresponsive, contorted, with no evident ability to interact with the environment? What human dignity remains here? Why should we not treat such human beings as we (properly) treat dumb animals, and put them out of "their misery"? I grant that one faces here the hardest case for the argument I am advancing. Yet one probably cannot be absolutely sure, even here, about the complete absence of inner life or awareness of their surroundings. In some cases, admittedly extremely rare, persons recover from profound coma (even with flat EEG); and they sometimes report having had partial yet vivid awareness of what was said and done to them, though they had given no external evidence of same. But beyond any restraint owing to ignorance, I would also myself be restrained by the human form, by *human blood*, and by what I owe to the full human life that this particular instance of humanity once lived. I would gladly stand aside and let die, say in the advent of pneumonia; I would do little beyond the minimum to sustain life; but I would not countenance the giving of lethal injections or the taking of other actions deliberately intending the patient's death. Between only undignified courses of action, this strikes me as the least undignified—especially for myself.

I have no illusions that it is easy to live with a Karen Ann Quinlan or a Nancy Cruzan or the baby Linares. I think I sufficiently appreciate the anguish of their parents or their children, and the distortion of their lives and the lives of their families. I also know that, when hearts break and people can stand it no longer, mercy killing will happen, and I think we should be prepared to excuse it—as we generally do—when it occurs in this way. But an excuse is not yet a justification, and very far from dignity.

What then should we conclude, as a matter of social policy? We should reject the counsel of those who, seeking to drive a wedge between human dignity and the sanctity of life, argue the need for active euthanasia, especially in the name of death with dignity. For it is precisely the setting of fixed limits on violating human life that makes possible our efforts at dignified relations with our fellow men, especially when their neediness and disability try our patience. We will never be able to relate even decently to people if we are entitled always to consider that one option before us is to make them dead. Thus, when the advocates for euthanasia press us with the most heart-rending cases, we should be sympathetic but firm. Our response should be neither "Yes, for mercy's sake," nor "Murder! Unthinkable!" but "Sorry. No." Above all we must not allow ourselves to become self-deceived: we must never seek to relieve *our own* frustrations and bitterness over the lingering deaths of others by pretending that we can kill them to sustain *their dignity*.

Coda

The ancient Greeks knew about hubris and its tragic fate. We modern rationalists do not. We do not yet understand that the project for the conquest of death leads only to dehumanization, that any attempt to gain the tree of life by means of the tree of knowledge leads inevitably also to the hemlock, and that the utter rationalization of life under the banner of the will gives rise to a world in which the victors live long enough to finish life demented and without choice. The human curse is to discover only too late the evils latent in acquiring the goods we wish for.

Against the background of enormous medical success, terminal illness and incurable disease appear as failures and as affronts to human pride. We refuse to be caught resourceless. Thus, having adopted a largely technical approach to human life and having medicalized so much of the end of life, we now are willing to contemplate a final technical solution for the evil of human finitude and for our own technical (but unavoidable) "failure," as well as for the degradations of life that are the unintended consequences of our technical successes. This is dangerous folly. People who care for autonomy and human dignity should try rather to reverse this dehumanization of the last stages of life, instead of giving dehumanization its final triumph by welcoming the desperate goodbye-to-all-that contained in one final plea for poison.

The present crisis that leads some to press for active euthanasia is really an opportunity to learn the limits of the medicalization of life and death and to recover an appreciation of living with and against mortality. It is an opportunity to remember and affirm that there remains a residual human wholeness—however precarious—that can be cared for even in the face of incurable and terminal illness. Should we cave in, should we choose to become technical dispensers of death, we will not only be abandoning our loved ones and our duty to care; we will exacerbate the worst tendencies of modern life, embracing technicism and so-called humaneness where encouragement and humanity are both required and sorely lacking. On the other hand, should we hold fast, should we decline "the ethics of choice" and its deadly options, should we learn that finitude is no disgrace and that human dignity can be cared for to the very end, we may yet be able to stem the rising tide that threatens permanently to submerge the best hopes for human dignity.

In Defense of Voluntary Euthanasia

Sidney Hook

Few American thinkers have attained the prominence of the late Sidney Hook. A professor of philosophy at New York University, Hook was engaged in virtually every important debate about social issues in the twentieth century. This op-ed piece appeared in the *New York Times* in March 1987.

A few short years ago, I lay at the point of death. A congestive heart failure was treated for diagnostic purposes by an angiogram that triggered a stroke. Violent and painful hiccups, uninterrupted for several days and nights, prevented the ingestion of food. My left side and one of my vocal cords became paralyzed. Some form of pleurisy set in, and I felt I was drowning in a sea of slime. At one point, my heart stopped beating; just as I lost consciousness, it was thumped back into action again. In one of my lucid intervals during those days of agony, I asked my physician to discontinue all life-supporting services or show me how to do it. He refused and predicted that some day I would appreciate the unwisdom of my request.

A month later, I was discharged from the hospital. In six months, I regained the use of my limbs, and although my voice still lacks its old resonance and carrying power I no longer croak like a frog. There remain some minor disabilities and I am restricted to a rigorous, low-sodium diet. I have resumed my writing and research.

My experience can be and has been cited as an argument against honoring requests of stricken patients to be gently eased out of their pain and life. I cannot agree. There are two main reasons. As an octogenarian, there is a reasonable likelihood that I may suffer another "cardiovascular accident" or worse. I may not even be in a position to ask for the surcease of pain. It seems to me that I have already paid

237

my dues to death—indeed, although time has softened my
memories they are vivid enough to justify my saying that I
suffered enough to warrant dying several times over. Why
run the risk of more?

Secondly, I dread imposing on my family and friends
another grim round of misery similar to the one my first
attack occasioned.

My wife and children endured enough for one lifetime. I
know that for them the long days and nights of waiting, the
disruption of their professional duties and their own familiar responsibilities counted for nothing in their anxiety for
me. In their joy at my recovery they have been forgotten.
Nonetheless, to visit another prolonged spell of helpless
suffering on them as my life ebbs away, or even worse, if I
linger on into a comatose senility, seems altogether gratu-
itous.

But what, it may be asked, of the joy and satisfaction of
living, of basking in the sunshine, listening to music, watching one's grandchildren growing into adolescence, following the news about the fate of freedom in a troubled world,
playing with ideas, writing one's testament of wisdom and
folly for posterity? Is not all that one endured, together with
the risk of its recurrence, an acceptable price for the multiple satisfactions that are still open even to a person of
advanced years?

Apparently those who cling to life no matter what, think
so. I do not.

The zest and intensity of these experiences are no
longer what they used to be. I am not vain enough to de-
lude myself that I can in the few remaining years make an
important discovery useful for mankind or can lead a social movement or do anything that will be historically
eventful, no less event-making. My autobiography, which
describes a record of intellectual and political experiences
of some historical value, already much too long, could be
posthumously published. I have had my fill of joys and
sorrows and am not greedy for more life. I have always

thought that a test of whether one had found happiness in one's life is whether one would be willing to relive it—whether, if it were possible, one would accept the opportunity to be born again.

Having lived a full and relatively happy life, I would cheerfully accept the chance to be reborn, but certainly not to be reborn again as an infirm octogenarian. To some extent, my views reflect what I have seen happen to the aged and stricken who have been so unfortunate as to survive crippling paralysis. They suffer, and impose suffering on others, unable even to make a request that their torment be ended.

I am mindful too of the burdens placed upon the community, with its rapidly diminishing resources, to provide the adequate and costly services necessary to sustain the lives of those whose days and nights are spent on mattress graves of pain. A better use could be made of these resources to increase the opportunities and qualities of life for the young. I am not denying the moral obligation the community has to look after its disabled and aged. There are times, however, when an individual may find it pointless to insist on the fulfillment of a legal and moral right.

What is required is no great revolution in morals but an enlargement of imagination and an intelligent evaluation of alternative uses of community resources.

Long ago, Seneca observed that "the wise man will live as long as he ought, not as long as he can." One can envisage hypothetical circumstances in which one has a duty to prolong one's life despite its costs for the sake of others, but such circumstances are far removed from the ordinary prospects we are considering. If wisdom is rooted in knowledge of the alternatives of choice, it must be reliably informed of the state one is in and its likely outcome. Scientific medicine is not infallible, but it is the best we have. Should a rational person be willing to endure acute suffering merely on the chance that a miraculous cure might presently be at hand? Each one should be permitted to make his own choice—especially when no one else is harmed by it.

The responsibility for the decision, whether deemed wise or foolish, must be with the chooser.

If You Love Her, Help Her Die

Betty Rollin

Betty Rollin is a contributing correspondent to NBC News. Her book about her mother's death, *Last Wish*, was made into a television movie. In this article, which first appeared in *Redbook* in July 1992, Rollin reflects on her experience and the way that it brought her into the assisted-suicide movement.

"Next to the happiness of my children, I want to die more than anything else in the world." My mother's words—unforgettable, searing, poignant in the extreme—spoken to me one late fall afternoon to convince me that she really meant it: She wanted to die, and would I please, please, help.

My mother had ovarian cancer. She endured chemotherapy and fought the good fight, and only when there was absolutely no hope, and nothing but disintegration and suffering ahead, did she decide she wanted out of life. With our help—my husband's and mine—she got out.

We didn't hand her a gun. If we had, we would have been prosecuted. Instead, we did research. We found out what it would take for her to die "safely." That may sound strange, but our main fear was that she would take pills that would only make her sicker and cause her more suffering without escape. But my mother got her doctor to write out the proper prescription, and she eased out of life as we hoped she would, and more important, as *she* hoped she would—painlessly, gracefully, gratefully. "I've had a wonderful life," she said to my husband and me during the last moments of her life. "I've had everything that is important to me. I've given love and I have received it. . . ."

I miss my mother, and I still get teary sometimes just thinking of her. These aren't tears of sadness, but of longing. I don't keep any photographs of my mother around. It tears me up to see her face—I miss her that much—and she's been gone almost ten years. But as much as I miss her, and as moved as I am by the memory of her death, it is not a painful memory. And that's because watching her die was like watching her go over a prison wall. Life for her had become a trap, she'd continually said, and she was grateful to escape. And my husband and I were grateful that she made it.

Over the years, in response to *Last Wish*, my book about my mother, and more recently, in response to a TV movie based on it, I've received hundreds and hundreds of letters from strangers. Mostly, the mail is supportive and empathetic, but as I open the envelopes, I always steel myself for the other kind. Now and then someone calls me a murderer. These few negative letters are from the sort of people who assume they know better than the rest of us how God feels. "Death by any person's hand is killing a life that God created," they write. But I still remember my mother's own view. "God gave me a brain," she said a few days before she killed herself, "and I'm glad it's still working so that I can die the way I want to."

The vast majority of letters are from people who have had the kind of experience that leads them to understand how she felt. A 40-year-old woman writes: "My mom died of multiple myeloma when she was forty-nine. I was seventeen at the time. Days before she lapsed into a coma, she asked me to help her die. She was then about eighty pounds and in terrible pain, and it was the worst moment of my life. I almost did it, but I was too scared. People who have never watched someone they love suffer should never judge the decision you make. I miss my mom, too."

From a young man whose companion is dying of AIDS: "He asked me to help him die and I want to, but how? I cannot find the strength to let go. But your story helps me."

From a young geriatric nurse: "I believe it's doctors who cannot deal with death. They put the feeding tube in and walk away feeling like heroes. They don't want to know that the patient can't talk, can't move, can't do anything for herself. I've had patients beg me to help them die. I support euthanasia. Talk to nurses in geriatrics. They know the truth."

The truth that nurse refers to is this: Some people at the end of life, who, even with the best medical efforts, cannot be made comfortable, desperately want to die. But they can't die without help. Even if they have access to the kind of drugs that would kill them, some people no longer have the ability to swallow. Or they're in a hospital, where if they took anything lethal, they'd wind up getting their stomach pumped. Or if they're home, they're with children or spouses who can't or won't help for whatever reason. (And I've had some heartbreaking letters from family members who *didn't* help and felt guilty forever.)

My heart goes out to these wives and husbands and children. Even I, who have never had a bad moment about helping my mother to die, was haunted by the "what-ifs." What if my mother had been unable to keep the pills down? What if we had been indicted? (Suicide by your own hand is not illegal in America, but assisting a suicide is.) And there's another, serious what-if: What if this were more *my* wish than hers? What if *I* had been tired of her life rather than she being tired of it?

For all of those reasons, I do *not* think family members should be the ones to help a desperate person die. It happened to work out in my family, but I cannot recommend the course of action we took for everyone. Instead, what we urgently need is a law that would allow physicians to carry out the wishes of a dying person.

So-called aid-in-dying laws must have safeguards, of course, as there were in the statute that was proposed—and narrowly defeated—in Washington State last year. There are even more safeguards in an initiative that will be voted on in California this November: The patient must be mentally competent, must be declared terminally ill by two physicians, and must be able to revoke the decision at any time.

My teacher in these matters is a soft-spoken lawyer

named Michael White, president of Americans Against Human Suffering, the group behind the initiative in California. After *Last Wish* aired on TV, he called and asked me to join him in addressing the policy-making branch of the American Bar Association. The object was to try to win the group's support for a proposal for physician aid in dying. I said yes and, with that phone call, went from journalist to activist—a leap I knew I'd make sooner or later, a leap I know my mother would have wanted me to make.

So last February I found myself in front of about 300 lawyers, telling them why they should support a resolution in favor of aid-in-dying legislation. "It's hard to imagine the kind of suffering that makes people beg to die," I said. "These are not people you normally see—unless they're someone you love."

The ABA voted the resolution down. But Michael White assured me that a larger purpose was accomplished: forcing people to think about this issue. *Not good enough*, I thought on the way home. *Not fast enough.*

I've been a reporter most of my working life—a passive commentator. I'm new at being involved. Maybe that's why I haven't learned patience. What's more, I've seen what suffering and helplessness look like up close. To me, this is an emergency.

As I write, I know there are people dying in hospital beds or (if they're more fortunate) at home. They're near the end of life, with nothing ahead but pain and terror. They want out and they can't get out. We must not turn our backs on these people. They have a right to die, if that's what they truly want.

Those opposed talk about God. But why assume a punishing, vindictive God who is against common sense? And as far as "interfering" with God's work, don't we "interfere" when we hook people up to respirators to *prolong* their lives? Isn't surgery interference?

Others opposed worry about possible abuses. If physician-assisted suicide is legal, can coercion be far behind? Will family members try to push their elderly relatives into taking a step they don't really want to take? This concerns me, too—and it concerns those who want the law changed. That's why safeguards aimed at preventing abuse are part of responsible aid-in-dying laws. Does it mean that abuse will never happen? Of course not. But to deny help to people because of a remote possibility of abuse is cruel.

Another benefit of legal aid in dying is to relieve fear. There is evidence to suggest that most patients, given the opportunity to end their lives, wouldn't. But knowing they have the option would be merciful in itself. When my mother knew we had found a way out for her, she became peaceful and unafraid. She felt in control. Even so, she felt she had to act while she was still able to swallow pills. So she took her own life at a moment that she felt relatively well. If she had had the security of knowing that it was legal for her doctor to give her a lethal shot later on, she would have waited. She would have lived longer.

My mother had a painless, dignified death. But I continue to hear from people denied that option, some of them begging me for a death recipe. Times have changed, because now I can at least recommend to them the Hemlock Society's book, *Final Exit,* for which I wrote an introduction. But ultimately, I can't help these people the way I helped my mother. What I *can* do is join the fight to change the law. It's going to be a state-by-state battle, and California is next up.

In my mother's memory, I plan to be there.

Life Is Sacred: That's the Easy Part

Ronald Dworkin

Ronald Dworkin is professor of law at New York University and professor of jurisprudence at Oxford University. He is one of the most influential contemporary commentators on social issues. This article first appeared in the *New York Times Magazine* in May 1993.

The fierce argument about abortion and euthanasia now raging in America is this century's Civil War. When Dr. David Gunn was shot and killed in front of a Florida abortion clinic last March, any hope that the abortion battle had finally become less savage died with him. The argument over euthanasia has been less violent but equally intense. When Nancy Cruzan was finally allowed to die in a Missouri hospital in 1991, after seven years in a persistent vegetative state, people called her parents murderers and her nurses wept over what was being done to her.

These terrible controversies have been far more polarized and bitter than they need and should have been, however, because most Americans have misunderstood what the arguments are *about.* According to the usual explanation, the abortion struggle is about whether a fetus, from the moment of conception, is already a person—already a creature whose interests other people must respect and whose rights government must protect. If that is the correct way to understand the debate, then of course accommodation is impossible; people who think that abortion violates a fetus's right to life can no more compromise than decent people can compromise over genocide.

But in fact, in spite of the scalding rhetoric, almost none of those who believe abortion may be objectionable on moral grounds actually believe that an early fetus is a person with rights and interests of its own. The vast majority of them think abortion morally permissible when necessary to save the mother's life, and only somewhat fewer that it is permissible in cases of rape and incest. Many of them also think that even when abortion is morally wrong, it is none of the law's business to prohibit it. None of this is compatible with thinking that a fetus has interests of its own. Doctors are not permitted to kill one innocent person to save the life of another one; a fetus should not be punished for a sexual crime of which it is wholly innocent, and it is certainly part of government's business to protect the rights and interests of persons too weak to protect themselves.

So conservative opinion cannot consistently be based on the idea that a fetus has interests of its own from the moment of conception. Neither can liberal and moderate opinion be based simply on rejecting that idea. Most liberals insist that abortion is always a morally grave decision, not to be taken for frivolous or capricious reasons, and this positive moral position must be based on more than the negative claim that a fetus has no interests or rights.

I suggest a different explanation of the controversy: We disagree about abortion not because some of us think and others deny, that an immature fetus is already a person with interests of its own but, paradoxically, because of an ideal we share. We almost all accept, as the inarticulate assumption behind much of our experience and conviction, that human life in all its forms is *sacred*—that it has intrinsic and objective value quite apart from any value it might have to the person whose life it is. For some of us, this is a matter of religious faith; for others, of secular but deep philosophical belief. But though we agree that life is sacred, we disagree about the source and character of that sacred value and therefore about which decisions respect and which dishonor it. I can best explain what the idea that life has intrinsic and objective value means by turning to the other agonizing controversy I mentioned, at the far edge of life.

Should a doctor prescribe enough pills to allow a patient with leukemia to kill herself, as Dr. Timothy Quill of Rochester did in 1991? Should he ever try to kill a patient in agony and pleading to die by injecting her with potassium chloride, as Dr. Nigel Cox did in Britain last year? Many people concede that in such terrible circumstances death would actually be in the patient's best interests, but nevertheless insist that killing her or letting her die would be wrong because human life has an independent, sacred value and should be preserved for that reason.

There is nothing odd or unusual about the idea that it is wrong to destroy some creatures or things, not because they themselves have interests that would be violated but because of the intrinsic value they embody. We take that view, for example, of great paintings and also of distinct animal species, like the Siberian tiger, that we work to save from extinction. Paintings and species do not have interests: if it nevertheless seems terrible to destroy them, because of their intrinsic value, it can also seem terrible to destroy a human life, which most people think even more precious, though that human life has not yet developed into a creature with interests either. So people can passionately oppose abortion for that reason even though they do not believe that a collection of growing cells just implanted in a womb already has interests of its own.

Once we identify that different basis for thinking abortion wrong, we see that it actually unites as well as divides our society, because almost everyone—conservatives, moderates and liberals on the issue of abortion—accepts both that the life of a human fetus embodies an intrinsic value and that a frivolous abortion is contemptuous of that important value. Americans disagree about when abortion is morally permissible, not because many of them reject the idea that human life is sacred but because they disagree about how best to respect that value when continuing a pregnancy would itself frustrate or damage human life in some other grave way: when a child would be born seriously deformed, for example, or when childbirth would frustrate a teen-age mother's chances to make something of her own life, or when the economic burden of another child would mean more privation for other children already living in poverty.

In such cases, respect for the inherent value of a human life pulls in two directions, and some resolution of the tragic conflict is necessary. How each of us resolves it will depend on our deeper, essentially religious or philosophical convictions about which of the different sources of life's sacred value is most important. People who think that biological life—the gift of God or nature—is the transcendently important source of that sacred value will think that the death of any human creature, even one whose life in earnest has not yet begun, is always the worst possible insult to the sanctity of life. Those who think that frustrating people's struggle to make something of their own lives, once those lives are under way, is sometimes an even greater affront to the value of life than an early abortion might resolve the conflict in the other direction.

That view of how and why we disagree about abortion also explains why so many people think that even when early abortion is morally wrong, government has no business forbidding it. There is no contradiction in insisting that abortion sometimes dishonors a sacred value and that government must nevertheless allow women to decide for themselves when it does. On the contrary, that very distinction is at the heart of one of the most important liberties modern democracies have established, a liberty America leads the world in protecting—freedom of conscience and religion. Once we see the abortion argument in this light, we see that it is an essentially *religious* argument—not about who has rights and how government should protect these, but a very different, more abstract and spiritual argument about the meaning and character and value of human life itself. Government does have a responsibility to help people understand the gravity of these decisions about life and death, but it has no right to dictate which decision they must finally make.

The same is true of euthanasia. Of course, any legal regime that permits doctors to help patients die must be scrupulously careful to protect the patient's real, reflective wishes and to avoid patients or relatives making an unwitting choice for death when there is a genuine chance of medical recovery. But government can do people great harm by not allowing them to die when that is their settled wish and in their best interests, as they themselves have judged or would judge their interests when very competent to do so.

In both cases, the crucial question is not whether to respect the sanctity of life, but which decision best respects it. People who dread being kept alive, permanently unconscious or sedated beyond sense, intubated and groomed and tended as vegetables, think this condition degrades rather than respects what has been intrinsically valuable in their own living. Others disagree: They believe, about euthanasia as about abortion, that mere biological life is so inherently precious that nothing can justify deliberately ending it. The disagreement, once again, is an essentially religious or spiritual one and a decent government, committed to personal integrity and freedom, has no business imposing a decision. Dictating how people should see the meaning of their own lives and deaths is a crippling, humiliating form of tyranny.

If we change our collective view of these two great controversies, if we realize that we are arguing not about whether abortion and euthanasia are murder but about how best to honor a humane ideal we all share, then we can cure the bitterness in our national soul. Freedom of choice can be accepted by all sides with no sense of moral compromise, just as all religious groups and sects can accept, with no sense of compromise, freedom for other versions of spiritual truth, even those they think gravely mistaken. We might even hope for something more: a healing sense, after all the decades of hate, that what unites us is more important than our differences. It is inevitable that free people who really do believe that human life is sacred will disagree about how to live and die in the light of that conviction, because free people will insist on making that profound and self-defining decision for themselves.

ACKNOWLEDGMENTS

Several people were crucial in helping me see this project through. Betsy Amster and Angela Miller were instrumental in helping me formulate the goals and shape the idea of the book. I owe a great deal to the energy and intelligence of my editors at Simon & Schuster: Mitch Horowitz, whose vision for *Arguing Euthanasia* kept me on course but who had to endure many telephone conversations in the process, and Andrew Stuart, who brought the project to completion.

Avaneda Hobbs typed the manuscript, and Marilyn Petralia helped me sort out the licensing issues. I am grateful to both of them. Thanks also to Marna Howarth of the Hastings Center for some last-minute bibliographic assistance.

My wife, Leslye Fenton, somehow found the time to relieve me of some parenting so that I could meet a few deadlines.

Arguing Euthanasia is dedicated to my mother, Zerka T. Moreno, a remarkable human being who lives her conviction that life is worth living, and is an inspiration for all who know her.

J. D. M.

ABOUT THE EDITOR

Jonathan D. Moreno, Ph.D., is Professor of Pediatrics and of Medicine and Director of the Division of Humanities in Medicine at the State University of New York Health Science Center at Brooklyn and an adjunct associate of the Hastings Center. A fellow of the Kennedy Institute of Ethics at Georgetown University and of the New York Academy of Medicine, he has served as a consultant on ethical issues for state and federal agencies and for several professional organizations. He is a frequent contributor to journals of bioethics and medicine and is the author of *Deciding Together: Bioethics and Moral Consensus*.